A History of Correctional Violence:
An Examination of Reported Causes of Riots and Disturbances

Reid H. Montgomery, Jr., Ph.D.

Gordon A. Crews, Ph.D.

FOUNDED 1870

American Correctional Association Staff

Reginald A. Wilkinson, *President*
James A. Gondles, Jr. , *Executive Director*
Gabriella M. Daley, *Director, Communications and Publications*
Leslie A. Maxam, *Assistant Director, Communications and Publications*
Alice Fins, *Publications Managing Editor*
Michael Kelly, *Associate Editor*
Sherry Wulfekuhle, *Editorial Assistant*
Dana M. Murray, *Graphics and Production Manager*

Cover by Michael Selby, *Graphics and Production Assistant*

Production by Design Consultants, Gainesville, VA
Printed in the United States of America by Graphic Communications, Inc., Upper Marlboro, MD.

ISBN 1-56991-078-2

This publication may be ordered from:
American Correctional Association
4380 Forbes Boulevard
Lanham, Maryland 20706-4322
1-800-222-5646

For information on publications and videos available from ACA,
contact our worldwide web home page at:
http://www.corrections.com/aca

Library of Congress Cataloging-in-Publication Data

Montgomery, Reid H.
     A history of correctional violence : an examination of reported
causes of riots and disturbances / Reid H. Montgomery, Gordon A.
Crews)
          p.   cm.
     Includes bibliographical references and index.
     ISBN 1-56991-078-2 (pbk.)
     1. Prison riots—United States.   2. Prison violence—United
States.   I. Crews, Gordon A.   II. Title.
HV9025.M66 1998
365'.641—dc21   98-13879
                                                                CIP

Table of Contents

"A society can be gauged by
how well it treats its prisoners."

Fyodor Dostoyevsky
Crime and Punishment, 1866

Dedication

Dr. Gordon A. Crews, Dr. Vernon Fox, Mr. William Crawley, and
Dr. Reid H. Montgomery, Jr.

This book is dedicated to the life, work, research, and teaching
of Dr. Vernon Fox, Professor of Criminology at the Florida State
University School of Criminology from 1952-1986. Dr. Fox
developed one of the first theories dealing with correctional
violence—The Time Bomb Theory of Prison Riots. Dr. Fox has
authored numerous books and journal articles dealing with
correctional issues. Many of his works have been translated and
used in numerous foreign countries.

Objectives

The authors' objectives for the readers of this book are the following:

- To combine advanced scholarship while communicating information to a wide audience

- To function beyond a basic resource on the causes of prison riots; we hope that it will offer new insights through our interpretations of many aspects of the complex processes involved in prison violence

- To inform the intelligent layperson and influence leaders of our society, including those practitioners and students of criminal justice, about prison riots and correctional violence in American society so that they can gain insights that will enable them to prevent or lessen such occurrences in the future

Acknowledgments

This book would not have been possible without the unwavering help of many people who were generous with their ideas as well as their time. The authors wish to thank the following people for their assistance and support:

The following members of the South Carolina Department of Corrections: Commissioner Michael Moore, Major Joseph D. McBride, Mr. Al Waters, Mr. George Roof, Mr. Ken McKellar, and the members of the South Carolina Department of Corrections' SWAT Team, for allowing us into their institutions and training sessions; Ms. Jennifer Cover for her editing and photography work; South Carolina Museum of Archives for allowing us the use of their collections; Ms. Alice Fins and Ms. Gabriella Daley of the American Correctional Association without whom this work would never have been possible; Dean Blease Graham, College of Criminal Justice, University of South Carolina for his support during the completion of this work; Dr. Gene Stephens, College of Criminal Justice, University of South Carolina, for allowing us to gain from his expertise on futuristic issues; Mr. Christopher Bruce Roberts, Criminal Justice Honors Student at Midlands Technical College, for his assistance in the research for this work; Dr. Chris Plyler and Associate Dean Lila Meeks, University of South Carolina Beaufort, for their support during the completion of this project; and last, but not least, our families and loved ones, Inez Montgomery, Jane Cauthen, Gordon and Joyce Crews, Paul and Jean Player, and Pamela, Garrison, and Samantha Crews, for making it all worthwhile.

R. H. M., Jr.
G. A. C.

Preface

The American Correctional Association has long had an interest in understanding and preventing violence within correctional facilities. We have published a number of materials on this topic, each of which adds to this purpose. Now, with this latest book, we have advanced another step. If you can teach those in corrections the warning signs of a riot, then administrators and staff are in a strong position to alleviate it or shorten its duration and intensity. And, if students of corrections learn what a riot is and how to detect unrest, they may be fortunate to never experience this kind of violence.

Based on this analysis of riots and disturbances, practitioners may be able to determine not only where a riot is likely to occur but when they are most vulnerable to the impact of a riot. Through proper education and training, especially in communication skills, as well as in the proper escalation of use of force, today's correctional staff may be able to de-escalate confrontational situations and, through leadership skills, defuse tensions.

Some of our reviewers scoffed at the authors' futuristic suggestions—but each day some of their visions are becoming reality. If we expand our paradigms, then we can develop new ways to prevent violence and lower its impact. By engaging in a dialog about these visions, we can develop present-day solutions that may be more innovative and doable than we had previously dared to believe. We should not be afraid of the future especially if we can help design it.

James A. Gondles, Jr.
Executive Director
American Correctional Association

Introduction

I s it time for Americans to become complacent once again? After all, recent
statistics, widely touted by the media, have suggested a small, albeit surprising,
drop in the rate of violent crimes committed in our nation during the past several
years. Nevertheless, the sobering fact remains that during the past decade, there has
been a significant rise in: (1) acts of domestic violence (Polusny and Folletee, 1996);
(2) violence in our schools (Crews and Counts, 1997; Warthen, 1997); (3) juvenile
violence, in general (Eron, Gentry and Schlegel, 1994; Loeber and Hay, 1997); (4) the
size of our state and federal prison populations (U.S. Department of Justice, 1997); and,
as is the subject of the present text, (5) riots in these same correctional institutions.

Of particular importance in this regard, the U.S. Department of Justice recently reported
a rather staggering 43 percent increase in the number of state and federal inmates
between 1990, a year in which approximately 716,000 individuals were serving time,
and 1995, when our prison population finally surpassed the one million mark (Bureau
of Justice Statistics, 1997a).

As a result of these disconcerting trends, correction officials have added over 200 new
state and federal prisons since 1990. Obviously, those in the know are making efforts to
redress this alarming trend. In addition, during this same time span, we have witnessed
a 200 percent increase in the number of our fellow citizens placed on probation and,
therefore, subject to correctional supervision (Bureau of Justice Statistics, 1997a).

Unfortunately, however, such efforts may be too little and, possibly, too late. For
example, according to the South Carolina Department of Corrections *1996 Annual
Report*, 33 percent of inmates released from prison during the first half of this decade

have been reincarcerated within three years! More prisons and more correctional officers have not served as an effective means for the rehabilitation of such offenders. There appears to be little optimism for the immediate future, notwithstanding state and federal proposals involving "two/three strikes" laws, tougher parole terms, and so forth. In particular, a recent *Corrections Compendium* survey (April, 1996) forecasted yet another 43 percent increase in the number of U.S. citizens who will be incarcerated by the year 2002.

The present text addresses one aspect of the perplexing dilemmas facing our correctional officials, namely the marked increase in prison riots during the past several years. In this text, Drs. Montgomery and Crews have provided the reader with a thorough and fascinating glimpse into prison riots in the United States during this century, paying particular attention to underlying causes and the so-called "trigger events" leading up to the riots. In addition, the authors discuss recent theories regarding the causes of prison violence and have attempted to relate theory to those being incarcerated today, relative to those of the past. As duly noted, we have a serious problem in this area, and we need serious solutions. Coming up with those solutions, however, will require a more holistic perspective than those presently available (Loeber and Hay, 1997).

From a *biopsychosocial perspective*, prison violence can be seen as but one manifestation of the increase in acts of aggression, especially those involving violence, in our society. Accordingly, we need to address our current understanding of the "roots" of aggression and violence, beginning with a consideration of biological "forces" that may predispose some individuals to engage in such behavior. Then, we will consider the psychological and societal "forces" that appear to play an even greater causal role in aggression, violence, and criminal behavior.

To begin, we will look at one of the most exciting and promising directions in the field of psychology today. It focuses on the biological determinants of behavior. Through the ever-increasing efforts of *biopsychologists*, we have gained an awareness of how specific chemical messengers in the nervous system ("neurotransmitters"), as well as hormones, mediate specific patterns of behavior. Moreover, we are acquiring increased knowledge regarding the role of specific brain structures in the expression of behavioral traits. Finally, a subfield of biopsychology, known as *behavioral genetics*, has provided evidence for an inherited predisposition for the ultimate development and expression of many behavioral traits and behavioral disorders.

A capsule summary of some recent findings relevant to prison violence would include each of the following:

(a) Abnormally low levels of the neurotransmitter, known as serotonin, have been correlated with aggressive behavior and acts of violence, including suicide (Nordstrom and Asberg, 1992; Saudou, et al., 1994; Siever and Trestman, 1993; Virkkunen and Linnoila, 1993).

(b) Elevated levels of testosterone have been implicated in provocation-induced acts of aggression and violence in males (Christiansen and Winkler, 1992; Dabbs, Carr, Frady, and Riad, 1995; Frank, Glickman and Licht, 1991).

(c) Abnormalities of the prefrontal cortex have been associated with acts of aggression, criminal violence, and antisocial personality and other impulse-control disorders, including those associated with attention deficits (Damasio et al., 1994; Powell, Buchanan, and Gibbs, 1990; Uylings et al., 1990).

(d) Numerous studies have provided evidence for a significant genetic influence on both antisocial behavior and criminality in adults, both in the United States and abroad. Thus, for example, males who have a first-degree relative (such as a parent or sibling) who meets the diagnostic criteria for antisocial personality disorder (APD) show an increased risk for developing antisocial personality disorder, a risk that cannot be accounted for by "shared environment" alone. And, in a similar vein, adopted children who eventually engage in criminal behavior are more likely to "share" their criminal tendencies with a biological parent than with the foster parents who reared them (American Psychiatric Association, 1994; Rose, 1995; Tellegen, Lykken, Bouchard, Wilcox et al., 1988). Such tendencies may reflect an inherited predisposition for an "impulsive temperament," which may set the stage for the later development of an aggressive lifestyle (Baron and Richardson, 1994).

While such biological variables may constitute a "risk factor" for the development and expression of aggression, violence, and criminal behaviors, such factors, at best, can account for only a small fraction of the variability of these behaviors in our society. Consequently, it is important to consider potential *psychological*, as well as *sociocultural*, risk factors. We now know that aggression and violent tendencies can be learned.

Beginning with the pioneering research of psychologist Albert Bandura and colleagues (such as Bandura, Ross, and Ross, 1961, 1963; Bandura, 1973), many studies indicate that observing violence "begets violence." Thus, it is well established that exposure to filmed violence can lead to later acts of violence and/or increased aggressiveness in children, adolescents, and young adults. Such effects not only have been documented under somewhat artificial, laboratory conditions, but also in field studies involving real-life situations (Bandura, 1983; Lefkowitz, Eron, Walder, and Huesmann, 1977).

Because behaviors can be acquired through observation and imitation ("modeling"), these findings are alarming, given that recent estimates suggest that the average American child, who watches two to four hours of television per day, probably will have witnessed 8,000 murders and an additional 100,000 acts of violence, often of a senseless or glorified nature, by the age of twelve (Eron, 1993; Huston, Donnerstein, Fairchild, Feshbach et al., 1992).

Moreover, several studies have demonstrated that exposure to aggressive pornography may lead to males acting more aggressively towards females and may have provided the "fuel" for the recent rise in "date rapes" (see, for example, Check and Gulolen, 1989). Additionally, as psychologist Leonard Berkowitz (1988, 1994a) has suggested, viewing acts of aggression may prime the individual to incorporate into his or her basic system of beliefs certain violent or aggressive "scripts;" that is, the individual may adopt a new attitude that certain situations require aggressive actions for their successful resolution.

Finally, and most unfortunately, many of today's children are being exposed to parental models of violence, in the form of either witnessing spousal abuse and/or being the targets of abuse themselves (Loeber and Ray, 1997; Widom, 1989). It is plausible that a child's temperament, which, as noted, may be influenced by genetic factors, actually elicits a pattern of parental neglect, rejection, and ultimately, abuse that, in turn, could foster the child's ultimate expression of violent aggression (see Loeber and Ray, 1997).

Nevertheless, as violence is not "universal" (Triandis, 1994), we must consider various societal or sociocultural variables that may be contributing to the growth of aggression and violence in America. In this regard, there has been a change in recent years of the "typical" inmates inhabiting our nation's correctional institutions. Specifically, today's inmate population appears to reflect many of the following characteristics:

- Youthful males

- A past history of parental neglect and/or abuse (Loeber and Ray, 1997; Widom, 1989)

- Substandard education, attention deficits, hyperactivity, and a history of unemployment (Loeber and Ray, 1997)

- Impoverishment and exposure to inappropriate role models, including those involved in the "gang subculture," a subculture that is particularly prominent in inner city areas and that is characterized by a sense of inflated self-esteem, a proclivity for abusing alcohol and other "disinhibiting" drugs, and an obsession with guns (Berkowitz, 1994b; Loeber and Ray, 1997)

- A lack of hope for the future and a sense of injustice, which are factors that have been implicated in one's desire to belong to a "gang" (see Loeber and Ray, 1997)

The latter two characteristics may be related to the fact that young black and Hispanic Americans are being incarcerated at a substantially greater, and thus, disproportionate, rate than are their Euro-Caucasian counterparts (Bureau of Justice Statistics, 1997a). This issue needs to be addressed, since a key to successful rehabilitation of our criminal offenders necessarily involves establishing a sense of hope and equal opportunity.

In addition, if offenders continue to see themselves as part of a gang—a suggestion that certainly appears plausible—then, it is likely that they will maintain their "gang mentality" when they are behind bars. As noted, this mentality is comprised of an inflated self-esteem, which is associated with an attitude that "If I want it, I'm entitled to it!" In addition, it is heavily influenced by the "script" that the most efficient means for getting one's way and resolving conflicts that interfere with that endeavor must necessarily involve aggression and violence. Given this mentality that has been shaped by many interacting forces and appears to be escalating in our society, is it surprising that when frustrating circumstances arise in our correctional institutions, the inmates' collective response often would entail aggression and violence that, in turn, could lead to all-out rioting? In any event, one can only hope that our increasing awareness of the potential biological, psychological, and sociocultural risk factors for aggression and violence can be used to implement more effective intervention strategies in various "at risk" communities throughout our nation, so that the alarming trends described in the present text might be reversed.

Charles M. Gibbs, Ph.D.
Professor of Psychology
Midlands Technical College
Columbia, South Carolina

Issues of Prison Violence in America

Introduction

The modern American correctional system seems to be fighting numerous battles ranging from the recent evolution of determinant sentencing to an exploding population problem. Yet, the most dangerous and costly phenomenon in the current penal system is the prison riot. The authors' aim is to bring broad amounts of information to the specific study of correctional violence. This book also covers prison riots and disturbances from 1900 to 1995.

> *"First came prisons, then came prison riots."*
>
> Dr. Vernon Fox, 1956

Riots and disturbances present a very serious problem for the American criminal justice system, and practitioners and policymakers need accurate knowledge regarding the modern correctional system and how to prevent riots and disturbances. Past efforts at "riot research" have not provided a comprehensive consideration of all available institutional riot information. Our effort is to focus on providing a direction from which new ideas may emerge for the resolution of problems that are intrinsic to prison riots.

The first correctional riot reportedly took place in Simsbury, Connecticut in 1774, in a prison that had been constructed over an abandoned mine in 1773 (Fox, 1972, p. 35). In the current century alone, more than 1,300 riots have occurred in American correctional institutions. These riots have cost the American public millions of dollars. Research suggests that the trend of prison disturbances continues to accelerate in terms of the numbers of riots and the numbers of inmates involved, the amount of violence, and monetary losses. These findings should compel us to make changes in the American prison system.

Methodology of Riot Research

Overview of Problems Surrounding Riots Research

Researchers face numerous problems as they begin to explore the social phenomenon of the prison riot. The first and perhaps most frustrating dilemma concerns the accuracy of reporting. How a situation finally is labeled is highly dependent on the individual who actually is responsible for reporting the "riot." One of the dominant methods for reporting current prison information assigns the labeling to the reporter. These reporters are often very different from each other with respect to training and experience and have not been brought under the guidance of a universal system. Lacking such an inclusive system leads to reported information that is highly arbitrary.

Other significant problems of riot research are the issues surrounding "societal values." These issues have an impact on the methodology involved in riot research. Levels of confidence in an overall data pool frequently begin to decline as temporal displacement (time after the riot) is considered. A classical example of this problem is evident as

> *Ruffin v. Commonwealth*—In 1871, a state judge had stated that "prisoners have no more rights than slaves." This statement was the catalyst for the hands-off period in which the Supreme Court refused to consider most corrections-oriented cases on the grounds that imprisoned individuals are best dealt with by institutional administrators, as they are the most qualified and most familiar with the prison environment. 62 Virginia 790 (1871) (21 Gratt, Roxbury *Dictionary of Criminal Justice*; D. Champion, 1996).

researchers examine the concept of "racial tension." In the early years of this century, such societal friction was reported much less frequently than it is currently. However, as most recognize, racial problems have plagued American society since its inception. This discrepancy in reporting can be attributed to the changes that occur in the public's mind-set over a long period of time.

Problems of temporal displacement also occur in the information age. With this new era, the availability of data relevant to prison riots has increased at an exponential rate. The intake of this immense amount of information into a data pool has a significant impact on any results or conclusions. As the result of so much information, the outcome often is skewed, reflecting the differences in information available from different time periods. The biggest impacts in this area have resulted from the advances in

communications and computer technology.
These improvements have created better systems for dissemination and storage of data.
However, before such techniques were available, collection of data on social phenomena
was more difficult to obtain and to assimilate.

Spatial displacement, while not as significant
a factor in methodological development, nevertheless leads to problems in the reliability of
reported data. Differences in geography
(states, regions, counties, and so forth) often
generate variations in both cultures and cus-
toms that properly may be reflected in
research of this type. An example of such variations are the classical differences between the
"North" and the "South." Reported information undoubtedly mirrors these differences,
and consequently, skews any conclusions
derived from this data.

Books in an inmate law library.
(South Carolina State Archives)

Adopted Methodology

With these methodological limitations considered, the authors developed a comprehensive data pool of reported prison and jail riots and disturbances from the years 1900 to
1995. During this time period, there were approximately 1,334 reported incidents of
prison and jail violence across the United States. This number was obtained by an
extensive examination of national reports, state and local reports, newspaper accounts,
and information provided by the *Corrections Compendium: The National Journal for
Corrections*.

The authors collected initial data from the South Carolina Department of Corrections'
national study *Collective Violence in Correctional Institutions: A Search for Causes* (1973).
This study examined incidents of correctional violence from 1900 to 1971 obtained by
interviewing or administering survey instruments to the fifty commissioners of corrections throughout the United States.

To produce findings that were most current, data also was collected from the *National
Survey of Prison Riots* conducted in 1984 by University of South Carolina Professors
Dr. Reid H. Montgomery, Jr. and Dr. Ellis MacDougall. This survey requested that the

departments of correction from the fifty states, the District of Columbia, and the Federal Bureau of Prisons provide any and all information about violent prison incidents that they had incurred between 1971 and December 31, 1983. Dr. Reid H. Montgomery, Jr. and Dr. Gordon A. Crews repeated this study in 1996, conducting a second *National Survey of Prison Riots*, which requested the same type of information for the years 1984 to 1995.

The authors intend to provide valid findings concerning correctional riots by employing the largest data pool feasible. This data pool includes reported correctional violence altercations that occurred in various levels of institutions, including: male and female prisons, jails, reformatories, and detention centers. Because of the large number of reported riots and disturbances discussed in this book, there is much information from which general observations and conclusions may be drawn. In addition, the use of time specific (month, year) data has been collected and incorporated with respect to the twentieth century and has produced a higher level of validity in the findings.

Definitions of Prison Riots

While the first American prison riot did not occur until 1774 in Simsbury, Connecticut, the term "riot" previously had described public incidents and defined a riot as "a violent disturbance of the public peace by three or more persons assembled for a common private purpose." English law responded to the problems that such outbreaks created by legislating the "Riot Act" in 1715. This law enlarged the definition of a riot by stating that "if twelve or more persons unlawfully assembled and disturbed the public peace, then they must disperse upon proclamation or be considered guilty of a felony."

Supreme Court cases such as *Fulwood v. Clemmer* (206 F.Supp. 370 [1962]), *Cooper v. Pate* (378 U.S. 546 [1964]), and *Wolff v. McDonnell* (418 U.S. 539 [1974]) instituted the principle that inmates retained constitutional rights and, therefore, they had the right to sue to protect these rights. Because of this movement, by 1982 the prison systems in more than forty states were functioning under court orders addressing crowding or conditions of confinement.

However, by the mid-1990s, the pendulum had begun to swing again in the opposite direction, with public sentiment against inmates intensifying. Campaigns were initiated to control inmate litigation and judicial intervention. Political and media attention became more centered on petty lawsuits filed by inmates (John W. Roberts, 1997).

In 1951, the case of *State v. Lustig* (New Jersey Superior Court, 13 N.J. Super. 149, 80A. 2d 309, 310) defined a riot as "an unlawful assembly which had developed to a stage of violence." This precedent ruling on what constituted a riot was later expanded by American courts to include the following definitions:

(1) An act or acts of violence by one or more persons that are part of an assemblage of three or more persons, which act or acts shall constitute a

clear and present danger of, or shall result in, damage or injury to the property of any other person or to the person of any other individual.

(2) A threat or threats of the commission of an act or acts of violence by one or more persons having, individually or collectively, the ability of immediate execution of such threat or threats, here the performance of the threatened acts or acts of violence would constitute a clear and present danger of, or would result in, damage or injury to the property of any other person or to the person of any other individual. 18 U.S.C.A. 2102(a) (*Black's Law Dictionary*, 1996, p. 1,327).

The social phenomenon of a riot is not entirely limited to the public sector within a society. Rather, it is present, and in all probability more likely to occur, within the settings of a correctional institution. Such occurrences may lead to loss of life, damage to property, and risk to public safety. The observation and study of prison unrest continues to reveal patterns in both prevention and response that must be examined.

The main problem seems to be that individual criminal justice agencies tend to be reactive rather than future-oriented in their decision-making operations ... there can be no meaningful regional or systemwide planning without individual agencies first being able to establish their own orderly, systematic, and continuous processes of setting objectives, anticipating the future, and bringing these anticipations to bear on critical present decisions. (Burt Nanus, Professor Emeritus, University of Southern California, School of Management, *Journal of Criminal Justice*, 1974).

Throughout the study of prison riots, experts have developed various definitions describing the elements of a "riot." The South Carolina Department of Corrections (1973) conducted a national study of American prison riots between 1900 and 1971. In this study, the definition of a riot was "an incident involving fifteen or more inmates and resulting in property damage and/or personal injury" (p. 23). The results of their findings produced a level of consistency when comparing statistics, such as numbers of inmates, time of the year, "cause," property damage, action taken to end the riot, and so forth. The resulting level of uniformity was innovative and has become a model for many studies as one of the first federally funded studies of riots.

However, one problem that emerged from the use of this definition was the omission of incidents across the nation that did not meet the "fifteen-inmate" criteria. A classic example was the May 2, 1946 "blast out" at the federal prison of Alcatraz. This was a significant event, as it required military intervention and forty-eight hours to subdue the uprising and regain control of the institution. Such an omission leaves out many other acts of violence and disorder, which may provide great insight into this area of research.

In 1996, the American Correctional Association, in *Preventing and Managing Riots and Disturbances*, suggested that there were three categories of violence and disorder that may occur within a correctional institution. These are an incident, a disturbance, and a riot (p. 17).

- A riot occurs when a significant number of inmates control a significant portion of the facility for a significant period of time.

- A disturbance is a step down from a riot in that there are fewer inmates involved, and there is no control or minimal control of any portion of the facility by inmates.

- An incident is then a step down from a disturbance in that one or a few inmates are involved and there is no control of any portion of the facility for any period of time by an inmate.

During a 1986 riot in an Oregon Prison, a correctional officer was taken hostage. During the retaking of the prison, the state used force. Correctional officers were ordered to defend themselves as they recaptured the institution by shooting their weapons at the ground in front of the prisoners when there was danger of an inmate attack. It was anticipated that this form of deterrence would show the state's seriousness and quell the riot quickly.

As a result of these efforts, one prisoner was shot in the leg, the correctional officer was rescued, and the riot was put down successfully. In the ensuing months after the riot, the wounded prisoner brought suit against the prison personnel, claiming that his civil rights had been violated and that he had been subject to cruel and unusual punishment.

The Supreme Court found on behalf of the prison workers, denoting that the infliction of pain in the process of restoring prison security does not violate the Eighth Amendment. This decision protected prison officials from liabilities for any resultant injuries to inmates during a riot, and further gave prison officials the legitimacy required to use forceful means to quell prison riots. *Whitley v. Albers*, 475 U.S. 312, 106 S.Ct. 1078 (1986).

These terms range from an occurrence, which is least severe in terms of damage, time, number of inmates, and frequency, to those of the greatest magnitude. We can hope that these new standards of observation will encourage a more complete system of reporting on behalf of prison officials. However, these terms are ambiguous, leaving a high level of discretion to the individual or institution actually doing the reporting. This overall classification system actually may prove to be misleading to the researchers examining this topic.

Because these discrepancies create much confusion in the current literature available on the subject, the authors have deviated from both previous classifications and use another model. To be inclusive of all data in terms of past research, the authors employ a broader definition to reduce the previous problem of omission. The definition, which best suits the objective of this research, and which has been employed in the analysis of the data presented in this book, is as follows: A riot transpires when administrators report the loss of positive control of part or all of a correctional institution's population for a consequential amount of time.

Triggering Events and Reported Causes

The authors originally presented data synthesis used in this study as a "cause" of a prison riot. However, they recognize that by the very nature of collective behavior, it is not reasonable to expect that such data is fully accurate. Rather, the perception of the individual or institution reporting the information is more likely to influence the determination of what is the "cause." Therefore, for the purposes of this study, the term "reported causes" are used to acknowledge such discrepancies.

> When people think of prison violence, more often than not, they think of a prison riot. Yet, prison riots are relatively rare events. More common are the day-to-day confrontations among inmates and between correctional officers and inmates. Many correctional administrators find this latter type of violence difficult to address (Stojkovic and Lovell, 1992).

After the compilation of information, the authors developed criteria and began a systematic analysis of the prison riot data. The analysis revealed twelve common "reported causes" of prison riots. However, for a more complete understanding of the causation of a prison riot, the authors note, while this is a "cause/reported cause," it is not necessarily *the cause*. Rather, it is a final manifestation of an underlying level of hostility and most likely long-growing frustration of the inmates. Causative factors are the foundation from which the motivation or momentum for a riot is derived. Such conditions then are realized in the environment through a "triggering event."

CHAPTER 2

Independent Causes
and Triggering Events
of Prison Violence

Introduction

I n the history of American correctional institutions, prison riots are not a new
phenomenon. This chapter and Chapter 3 review information from past studies of
prison riots, specifically riots between the years 1900 and 1995. National surveys
from this time frame (South Carolina Department of Correction's *Collective Violence
Study, 1900-1971; National Study of Prison Riots; 1971-1983,
National Study of Prison Riots, 1984-1995; Corrections
Compendium,* and so forth) reported 1,334 riots across the
United States. The authors pooled the information generated by these studies to provide a secondary analysis that
offers pertinent data. This analysis revealed that the number one reported cause of prison violence was a confrontation between inmates. Other reported causes of prison
riots dealt with issues of racial tension, institutional food,
and multiple factors.

> *"We are men!
We are not beasts
and do not intend
to be beaten or
driven as such!"*
>
> Elliot James Barkley
> Attica Prison
> September 9, 1971

With the billions of tax dollars that are spent on corrections
each year and the large number of citizens who derive their employment from this
field, a prison riot could take a devastating toll on a jurisdiction that experiences a
major uprising. The authors seek to provide a more in-depth understanding of the
causes of prison riots.

Examples of Reported Single Causes of Prison Violence

Institutional Food

Three times a day across America, inmates are served food. Inmate dissatisfaction with institutional food is a potential "cause" of a pending riot. Hoarding of institutional food also can be a sign that inmates are preparing for a riot. Inmates who know that a riot is imminent may save food ahead of time (American Correctional Association, 1996). During a riot, food often can become a scarce item but one that is in great demand.

Food trays at a prison in South Carolina.
(*Source:* South Carolina State Archives)

Reports on numerous prison riots contend that they were caused by conflicts over institutional food. An early example can be found on a prison farm in Florida on March 11, 1927. Inmates rioted in a dispute over whether candy or cabbage should be included in their diet. During the riot, one correctional officer was taken hostage.

Another food-related prison riot took place on September 1, 1981, at the Washington State Penitentiary (Walla Walla, Washington). The riot broke out in the kitchen unit when the main food-serving line ran out of a food item. The riot lasted two hours and resulted in $491,114 worth of damages. There were several minor inmate injuries, and some staff were overcome by smoke. Correctional staff eventually used force to end the riot.

The following examples illustrate specific food-related demands of prisoners. Fifty-two inmates were involved in a prison riot at the Texas State Prison on April 15, 1955. The inmates demanded that they be served three meals a day instead of two meals. The riot lasted a total of thirty hours. The Bexar County Jail in Texas was the scene of a disturbance on January 12, 1957. Eighty inmates took part in the disturbance which arose because there had been no pancakes served at their breakfast meal. On August 1, 1962, a disturbance took place at the Youth Corrections Center in Washington, D.C. The forty inmates who took part in the riot, mostly Black Muslims, were upset with how the food was being prepared. The disturbance ended when the warden agreed not to cook pork.

The quality of institutional food was the cause of the riot that occurred on June 23, 1986, and involved forty-one inmates at the Kentucky State Penitentiary in Eddyville, Kentucky. In the three hours that the riot lasted, the entire law library and all its books were destroyed by fire. The laundry also was damaged badly, and three correctional officers and two inmates were injured. The riot ended when an emergency squad gained control by breaking inmates into small groups. Shots fired by the riot squad also were used to quell the situation.

Figure 2.1. Further Examples of Riots Caused by Institutional Food

Date	Institution	Consequences
June 5, 1952	Central Prison (NC)	150 inmates involved Lasted 6 hours Hostages taken
Sept. 12, 1952	Chillicothe Reformatory (OH)	40 inmates involved
Oct. 31, 1952	Ohio Penitentiary (OH)	$1,000,000 in damages
Apr. 12, 1953	Stillwater State Prison (MN)	1,018 inmates involved
Sept. 23, 1954	Missouri State Penitentiary (MO)	300 inmates involved Damage between $3 and $5 million
Sept. 26, 1954	Bridewell Prison (IL)	1,300 inmates involved Ended when 970 inmates were celled and promised improved meals
Nov. 6, 1971	Los Angeles (CA)	Lasted 4 1/2 hours
Oct. 16, 1989	FDC Oakdale (LA)	1,113 inmates participated

Analysis of Institutional Food

As these examples reflect, the demand for "special" diets is often a reported cause of prison and jail riots. When riots occur, the rioters' demands often are similar to the demands at Attica in 1971, "give us a healthy diet, stop feeding us so much pork, and give us some fresh fruit daily." Many inmate complaints center around food—such as too little food, not a good variety of food, no raw vegetables nor fresh fruit, not enough time for meals, food does not meet medical or religious requirements, or food has insects in it (American Correctional Association, Committee on Riots and Disturbances, 1990a).

To lessen the tension often generated by such objections, the American Correctional Association employs many standards for the operation of correctional facilities, including the accreditation of food service operations even when the rest of the institution is not accredited. Here are examples of some of these standards as they apply to institutional food service (American Correctional Association, 1990b and 1998).

The famous Supreme Court case, *Wilson v. Seiter* began in 1991 when an Ohio inmate named Wilson filed suit against the Hocking Correctional Facility's administrators, alleging that his Eighth and Fourteenth Amendments had been violated because of exposure to poor prison conditions. His list of complaints included deficient climate control, filthy and defective restrooms, unsuitable airing of cellblocks, extreme noise-levels, contaminated food preparation, unsanitary dining facilities, and lack of segregated/protective housing.

Wilson's suit was determined to be insufficient by the Supreme Court, which held that penitentiary/jail authorities must display intentional indifference to prisoner needs and living conditions in order for inmates to have valid claims in the eyes of the law. *Wilson v. Seiter*, 501 U.S. 294, 111 S.Ct. 2321 (1991).

Menu Planning (3-4298): Written policy, procedure, and practice require that food service staff plan menus in advance and substantially follow the plan, and that the planning and preparation of all meals take into consideration food flavor, texture, temperature, appearance, and palatability.

Dining Time (3-4151): Dining space is sufficient to serve all inmates in four or fewer shifts per meal while giving each inmate the opportunity to have at least twenty minutes of dining time for each meal.

Medical Diets (3-4299): Written policy, procedure, and practice provide for special diets as prescribed by appropriate medical or dental personnel.

Religious Diets (3-4300): Written policy, procedure, and practice provide for special diets for inmates whose religious beliefs require the adherence to religious dietary laws.

Sanitation and Hygiene (3-4154): Toilet and washbasin facilities are available to food service personnel and inmates in the vicinity of the food preparation area.

Because of the high potential for riots over food, many administrators encourage their staff to take the American Correctional Association Correctional Food Service Correspondence Course (1996a), which is equivalent to forty hours of in-service training.

Racial Tension

Race long has been involved in prison riots. For example, on July 25, 1920, the Bedford Reformatory for Women (Bedford, New York) reported a prison riot . This riot involved

150 inmates and lasted one hour. The reported cause was racial tension. The riot ended after twenty-five state police used clubs to restore order.

On July 10, 1952, a prison riot occurred at the St. Louis, Missouri Jail. This riot was caused when prison officials forced black and white inmates to eat dinner together. Five hundred inmates participated in this riot.

Eighty inmates participated in a prison riot at the Texas Ruck State Hospital on April 17, 1955. This six-hour riot was triggered by black inmates' demands that a recreation area be provided to them, as it had been for white inmates. Three prison staff members were held hostage. Five correctional officers and eight inmates were injured.

On December 3, 1970, the Kentucky Reformatory exploded into a riot. The riot involved 200 prisoners. The inmates caused $2,000 worth of damages to the institution. The reported cause was the integration of dormitories.

Another prison riot took place at the Kentucky State Reformatory in LaGrange, Kentucky, on August 6, 1972. This riot involved approximately 700 inmates. The reported cause of this riot was racial friction. No hostages were taken in this riot, but twenty-seven inmates and one officer were injured. The property damages included broken dormitory windows. The riot lasted two and one-half hours and ended when force was used to restore order.

On May 18, 1975, a prison riot took place at the maximum-security unit of the Colorado State Penitentiary (Canon City, Colorado). It involved approximately 250 inmates. It was caused by racial tension between black and Hispanic inmates. One Hispanic inmate was held hostage by black inmates, and two black inmates were held hostage by Hispanic inmates. One inmate was killed and several other inmates were injured. No staff were injured. The riot was ended after five hours by the use of force.

On June 24, 1978, a prison riot took place at the Georgia State Prison in Reidsville, Georgia. The cause was classified as a racial conflict. The riot involved approximately 300 inmates. No hostages were taken, no correctional officers were injured, and no inmates were harmed. The riot was ended by a show of force on the part of the administration.

> The Alabama prison system practiced prison segregation by race in the early 1960s. Black prisoners were separated from the white prisoners, and each group was treated differently. A suit was brought by the prisoners against the institution on the basis of racial discrimination. The Supreme Court stated that the Alabama correctional system indeed was acting in an unconstitutional manner as it violated the Fourteenth Amendment by housing prisoners separately based on their race. *Lee v. Washington*, 390 U.S. 333, 88 S.Ct. 944 (1968).

On May 9, 1981, a disturbance broke out at the Holman Prison in Atmore, Alabama. Racial conflict was reported between inmates in the prison. The disturbance started when a white inmate attempted to stab a black inmate who had been harassing him. A group of black inmates retaliated. The disturbance involved sixty inmates and lasted twenty minutes. Three inmates were stabbed during the disturbance. Property damage to furniture and windows amounted to $500. The disturbance ended when the Department of Corrections Riot Arrest Team separated the "ring leaders." Also, certain problematic inmates were locked down.

The Minnesota Correctional Facility in Stillwater, Minnesota, had a prison riot on September 11, 1983. The reported cause was a confrontation between white and black inmates. Officials estimated between twenty-two and forty inmates were involved in this riot, which lasted two hours. More than $20,000 worth of property was damaged, and the majority of this cost was from cells set on fire. Four inmates and one correctional officer were injured. Tear gas was used to end the riot.

Race was a reported cause for a prison riot at the Mack Alford Correctional Center in Stringtown, Oklahoma. The riot began on May 13, 1988 and ended on May 16. The riot ensued when inmates became disruptive over a series of thefts. Two groups of inmates, who were racially divided, accused each other of stealing. Eight hostages were taken in the riot. Over $7 million of damage was done to state property. A correctional officer was stabbed in the hand when he tried to hold a door closed against a group of rioting inmates. When correctional officials agreed to review inmate demands, the hostages were released, and the inmates surrendered.

Figure 2.2. Further Examples of Riots Caused by Racial Tension

Date	Institution	Consequences
May 2, 1953	Alcatraz (CA)	39 federal prisoners involved
Nov. 23, 1970	Cummins Prison Farm (AR)	500 inmates involved Lasted 2 days
July 23, 1978	Georgia State Prison (GA)	100 inmates involved 3 deaths resulted
Sept. 23, 1975	Colorado State Penitentiary (CO)	38 inmates involved
Sept. 4, 1992	MICC-Annex (WA)	112 inmates involved
Dec. 20, 1992	Hartford (CT)	30 inmates involved
Oct. 16, 1989	FDC Oakdale (LA)	1,113 inmates participated

Analysis of Racial Tensions

As race relations become a more important factor in the modern penal system, administrators must take steps to alleviate potentially destructive results. One correctional management technique to relieve racial tension which may be used is the proper classification of inmates. Many aggressive inmates will use race relations as a "justification" for violence. A classification system will separate inmates based on their aggressiveness and security risk. The classification technique can be a valuable management tool for correctional staff. An effective classification system that separates both individuals and groups based on some institutional-based type of criteria will help to minimize potential violence. The sys-

Inmate at work in South Carolina prison industries. Planned meaningful work holds down tensions. (*Source:* South Carolina State Archives)

tem allows correctional officers the discretion to request an inmate's reclassification if they observe inmate behavior that is uncharacteristic of the inmate's present classification (American Correctional Association, 1996b).

Another effective practice to employ in an institution to prevent riots caused by race relations or for other reasons is the use of meaningful programs for inmates. These programs should involve inmates in education, vocational training, jobs, career planning, counseling, and recreational activities. Simply confining inmates with little or no program or recreational activity can lead to excessive idleness, and idleness leads to time to plan ways to defeat the system—either through riots or other prohibited behavior. When inmates are busy, they spend less time arguing or fighting with other inmates or taking part in illegal activities, such as plotting escapes or riots. Useful programs also can improve inmates' self-esteem and help them prepare for their return to society (American Correctional Association, 1990a).

The American Correctional Association standards (1990b and 1998) offer guidance to reduce problems that may arise concerning inmate race issues. The following are some of the applicable standards that, if followed, may lessen racial tension.

Classification Plan (3-4282): Written policy, procedure, and practice provide for a written inmate classification plan. The plan specifies the objectives of the classification system and methods for achieving them, and it provides a monitoring and evaluation mechanism to determine whether the objectives are being met. The plan is reviewed at least annually and updated, as needed.

Level of Custody (3-4283): The classification system specifies the level of custody required and provides for a regular review of each classification.

Classification Status Reviews (3-4288): The classification plan specifies criteria and procedures for determining and changing an inmate's program status; the plan includes at least one level of appeal.

Access to Programs and Services (3-4265): Written policy, procedure, and practice prohibit discrimination based on an inmate's race, religion, national origin, sex, disability, or political views in making administrative decisions and in providing access to programs.

Inmate Work Plan (3-4394): The institution maintains a written plan for full-time work and/or program assignments for all inmates in the general population.

Rules, Regulations, and Policies

On occasion, inmates react to rules, regulations, and policies of prisons by rioting. For example, fifty inmates created a disturbance on April 3, 1916, at the Bronx County Jail in New York due to curtailment of visiting privileges.

In 1923, a special South Carolina joint legislative committee reported to the General Assembly on a riot which took place in the state penitentiary during the month of May, 1922. The report stated:

Recently, what was termed a riot broke out at the state penitentiary. From all testimony, both of prisoners and others, a number of convicts walked out from work with knives and sticks in their hands. They were in a threatening mood. The Columbia Fire Department, the Columbia Police, and the Sheriff of the county were called on for aid. County officers and penitentiary guards rushed around the corner of the building and opened fire upon the prisoners, none of whom was nearer than thirty-five yards to the officers. No order was given to fire, though the Superintendent of the penitentiary was with the charging party. It is evident that the officers armed with rifles and pistols were not in imminent danger from the men who were armed with small knives and sticks thirty-five yards away.

Riot scene at Kirkland Correctional Institution, Columbia, South Carolina. (South Carolina Department of Corrections – Mr. Al Waters' Collections)

In this affair a number of prisoners were wounded and one was killed. A cool, intelligent handling of the matter would have easily prevented this deplorable incident.

It is the committee's conviction that the cause of this fatal encounter was unnecessarily harsh punishment and disregard for rights to certain personal possessions long established by reasonable and safe custom. Under a properly disciplined force it could have been handled without promiscuous firing into a crowd of for the most part unarmed prisoners. Where lax methods of administration go hand in hand with harshness disturbances naturally follow. Stern discipline is of course necessary in handling the miscellaneous population of a state prison. Maudlin sentiment should have no place there, as desperate men as society produces are from time to time found there. The problems are very real and difficult and not for laymen; only men of experience and wisdom and character can handle them. So we have not expressed criticism without weighing our own words so as to state the plain, outstanding facts that any man of common sense would recognize (South Carolina, 1923, p. 1).

Thus, inmate disagreement with prison rules, regulations, and policies can boil over into a riot.

A disturbance occurred at the Indiana Reformatory (Pendleton Correctional Facility, Pendleton, Indiana) on July 2, 1956. This disturbance involved 300 inmates and lasted 30 minutes. The reported cause was the flogging of seven inmates in solitary confinement. Four staff members were held hostage. Eight inmates and two correctional officers were injured.

A prison riot took place at the Deep Lake Correctional Facility in Florida on February 8, 1957. This riot involved twenty-six inmates and lasted seven hours. The reported cause was conflict with the actions of correctional officers. The day prior to this riot, inmates had been denied a fifteen minute work-break. This anger evolved into a riot the following day.

The Hawaii State Prison had a riot in October of 1973. The triggering cause was an inmate's refusal to take medication. This forty-eight hour riot involved two hundred inmates. Property damage was approximately $600,000. There were no major injuries to inmates or staff. The riot ended by means of voluntary surrender.

A prison riot took place at the North Carolina Correctional Center for Women in Raleigh, North Carolina, on June 15, 1975. The reported cause was the demand by inmates for increased rights. Specifically, they cited six demands: (1) getting speedier hearings on grievances, (2) making improvements in medical care, (3) firing of some prison personnel, (4) forming of an inmate advisory board, (5) discontinuing of the prison laundry, and (6) promoting the acting superintendent to a permanent role. A total of 150 inmates out of the 500 incarcerated at this institution took part in the riot. No hostages were taken during the five-day period. Property damages included one dormitory fire, broken windows, and destroyed furniture. Force was used to end the riot after negotiations did not produce a peaceful resolution.

On July 11, 1981, a riot was reported at the DeSoto Correctional Institution in Arcada, Florida. The riot ensued after an inmate's television was turned off. Several hundred inmates took part in this riot, which resulted in injuries to twenty-five inmates. No staff were injured or taken hostage; however, property damages amounted to $61,736. The riot lasted an hour and fifty minutes and was ended by the use of force.

Another example of a riot over rules and regulations occurred at the Virginia State Penitentiary (Richmond, Virginia) on August 1, 1977. It involved two hundred inmates and lasted nine hours. The riot was triggered by a peaceful work stoppage, which turned violent. Inmates felt they had no way to communicate their concerns. The riot did not produce any injuries. It was ended by a show of force by the authorities.

The Maryland Correctional Institution in Hagerstown, Maryland, had a riot on May 15, 1990. Inmates were dissatisfied with the commissary and had significant complaints about the classification process, as well as the medical services. A total of 559 inmates were involved in this eight-and-a-half-hour riot. Four staff received minor injuries. Negotiation was used to end this riot.

On August 21, 1991, a prison riot took place at the Federal Correctional Institution in Talladega, Alabama. Approximately 120 Cuban detainees took part in this riot, which was caused by their scheduled repatriation to Cuba. Eleven staff were taken hostage in this riot. One hostage received minor injuries. No inmates were injured in the proceedings. However, there was extensive damage to a high-security living unit. The riot ended on August 30, 1991, when the Federal Bureau of Investigation and the Bureau of Prisons staged a predawn assault on the living unit. Explosives were used to blow open the entrance door. The detainees, who had been asleep, were caught off guard.

On April 17, 1995, inmates at the Broad River Correctional Institution in Columbia, South Carolina, rioted. The reported cause was a new hair policy, which governed the length of inmate's hair. Seven inmates, who were members of the "5 Percenters Gang," (a prison gang originating in the southeast United States) initiated the riot. Five correctional officers were stabbed, and rioters took three hostages. This riot ended after eleven hours when inmates were given the opportunity to meet with the news media. Damages from the riot totaled $10,000. Two hundred inmates took part in this riot.

Figure 2.3. Further Examples of Riots Caused by Rules, Regulations, and Policies

Date	Institution	Consequences
June 15, 1953	New Mexico Penitentiary (NM)	21 hostages taken 2 inmates killed
Sept. 21, 1971	Orleans Parish Prison (LA)	250 inmates involved Lasted 5 hours
May 3, 1975	Iowa State Penitentiary (IA)	19 inmates involved Caused $5000 in damages Lasted 5 hours
Mar. 15, 1985	St. Clair Correctional Facility (AL)	Lasted 10 hours 32 hostages taken
Aug. 25, 1993	Huntingdon (PA)	12 inmates involved
Aug. 27, 1993	Altona (NY)	500 inmates involved

Analysis of Rules, Regulations, and Policies

While the previous examples have expressed various reactions that may occur from inmates' conflict with the rules and regulations of an institution, the American Correctional Association (1996b, p. 111) has established three primary areas where the violation of rules, regulations, and policies actually may indicate the potential for a future riot.

The first of these indicators may be a high volume of weapons found during searches of inmates and their cells. Such discoveries of the stockpiling of weapons may be a significant indicator that the inmates are preparing for a prison riot. Second, often when drastic increases in the number of inmates signing up for "sick call" (medical call) occurs, the inmates may be faking illnesses because they know there is a pending riot and do not want to be in the institution during the violence. The third clue of impending riots is a significant increase in the number of inmates attempting to be placed into protective custody. They may do this to avoid being around the area where a riot or disturbance may occur. These inmates may be the "snitches" and "informants" who are targeted by instigators during riots, or they may be inmates who do not want to participate because they are "short-timers" (American Correctional Association, 1996b).

Keep in mind that inmates' perceptions of events that violate institutional regulations and policies may be very different from those of the administration. This difference in perception, while not completely resolvable, can be elevated somewhat by employing a policy that treats the inmates fairly, firmly, consistently, and equally. This type of interaction can aid in the decrease of tension within an institution, and indirectly prevent prison violence and possibly riots.

Another important skill that prison officials must possess is the ability to handle inmates' complaints and requests properly. Because of the close contact between inmates and correctional officers, it is possible to solve many of the problems and complaints at the base level, before they escalate into prison riots. However, for this prevention technique to be effective, correctional officers must have the training and authority to solve such problems (American Correctional Association, 1996b). The following list consists of procedural examples from the American Correctional Association standards (1990b and 1998) that are intended to curb possible problems in the area of rules, regulations, and policies.

> *Rules of Conduct* (3-4217): All personnel who work with inmates receive sufficient training so that they are thoroughly familiar with the rules of inmate conduct, the rationale for the rules, and the sanctions available.

Grievance Procedures (3-4271): There is a written inmate grievance procedure that is made available to all inmates and that includes at least one level of appeal.

Disciplinary Reports (3-4220): Written policy, procedure, and practice provide that when rule violations require formal resolution, staff members prepare a disciplinary report and forward it to the designated supervisor.

Conduct of Hearing (3-4228): Written policy, procedure, and practice provide that disciplinary hearings on rule violations are conducted by an impartial person or panel of persons. A record of the proceedings is made and maintained for at least six months.

Mass Escape Attempts

The escape motive may be the cause of many more riots than is reported. A riot often may be a distraction used to camouflage prisoners' escape plans. Many riots have been reported where inmates began a riot and then released other inmates to increase the chaos and size of a violent incident. In other cases, the idea of an escape attempt has materialized only after a riot has begun and sufficient momentum has been generated to make the escape possibility a reality. For example, on May 2, 1946, six inmates at the Alcatraz Federal Prison in California rioted and then escaped to freedom. The riot started when two inmates attacked a correctional officer to steal his keys. However, he managed to hide the key that would have facilitated the escape. Other officers were attacked, and their weapons were taken. A standoff between the six inmates and prison officials soon developed. Military units from the surrounding San Francisco area arrived to assist in regaining control of the institution. The riot ended when grenades were lowered into a utility corridor where the inmates were hiding. Three inmates were killed, and three more were taken into custody. Two correctional officers died in this riot, which lasted for forty-eight hours.

> In the past five years, according to research by Newhouse News Service, at least 117 killers have escaped. During that time, escapees have killed at least 25 people. . . . This year, if past figures are a guide, 11,000 inmates will escape in the United States— one every 45 minutes. (*Patriot News*, October 24, 1995).

On October 28, 1952, 363 inmates attempted to escape from the Menard State Prison in Menard, Illinois. The riot which resulted lasted five days and involved the holding of seven hostages.

On July 30, 1960, a prison riot took place at the Oahu State Prison in Hawaii. This riot involved seventy inmates and lasted five hours. The reported cause was an escape attempt.

On February 17, 1966, a disturbance took place at the Indiana Girls School Institution (Indianapolis Juvenile Correctional Facility, Indianapolis, Indiana). The reported cause was a distraction for a planned breakout. Thirty-five inmates took part in this disturbance, which resulted in injuries to eleven.

One of the duties of a correctional officer is to prevent escape attempts. On December 11, 1971, correctional officers at the District of Columbia Corrections Complex, located in northern Virginia, fired shots at inmates who were using a riot as an opportunity to escape. A similar riot took place at the Raiford State Prison in Florida on November 29, 1971.

On June 30, 1976, thirty-three inmates attempted to escape from the McDowell County Unit in Marion, North Carolina. Inmates hoped that by setting a fire in their unit they could carry out their plans to escape. Unfortunately, eight inmates died and twenty suffered smoke inhalation. There was approximately $25,000 worth of damage in the unit. The disturbance lasted only ten minutes. The riot ended in voluntary surrender as a result of the fire.

A prison riot took place on January 23, 1983 at the Cross City Correctional Institution in Florida. The triggering cause of this riot was the shooting of an inmate in an escape attempt. Approximately 200 inmates began to riot after the shooting. Damages to the institution from this four-hour riot amounted to $81,451.03. Force was used to end the riot.

Another disturbance took place at the Indiana State Prison on October 17, 1994, in Michigan City, Indiana. The cause was an escape attempt by five inmates on death row. The disturbance only lasted one hour. The significant damage was $4,000 in cut bars. The situation ended when a tower correctional officer fired a shot in concert with forceful restraint of offenders by an emergency squad. Of the fifty staff involved, only one was injured with a bruised knee, and no inmates were injured.

Figure 2.4. Further Examples of Riots Caused by Mass Escape Attempts

Date	Institution	Consequences
April 22, 1905	Central Correctional Institution (SC)	Death of captain of the guards 6 inmates involved
Dec. 9, 1952	New Mexico State Penitentiary (NM)	Lasted 20 hours 8 hostages taken
Oct. 31, 1970	Cummins Prison Farm (AR)	4 hostages taken Lasted 13 hours
July 16, 1971	Nebraska State Penitentiary (NE)	Property damages to cells, windows Lasted 1 1/2 hours
April, 1982	Maryland Penitentiary (MD)	5 staff taken hostage

Analysis of Mass Escape Attempts

The possibility of a mass-escape attempt is a realistic concern in any situation involving prison violence. Staff must take precautions prior to an uprising to insure that escape will not be possible, even during a prison riot. Prison officials must be conscious of three areas: floor plans, schematics, and operating procedures. All correctional officers must have knowledge of floor plans and exits in each institution. This will enable them to identify water valves, electricity, and heat controls. This knowledge not only will prove to be a useful tool in controlling the expansion of a prison siege, but may facilitate the retaking of an institution, or the minimization of institutional damage as a riot is terminated.

Knowledge of these schematics also may prove valuable before an emergency occurs. This will allow correctional and emergency staff to move quickly, efficiently, and safely to potentially halt a situation before it gets out of hand or spreads into additional areas of the institution. For example, during an evacuation, a staff member's knowledge of schematics may facilitate moving staff and inmates into areas of greater control or away from a potentially dangerous situation.

Properly implemented operating procedures also may prove invaluable to the prevention of mass escape attempts from penal institutions. History has proven this lesson to be a painful one, as many lives have been lost when such procedures were disregarded. Such operating procedures should be used to check and update environmental facilities (such as checking worn-out locks, checking the ground perimeter, and so forth).

When these types of policies are implemented and practiced on a regular basis, an institution's security level is increased exponentially. In line with these security concepts, the American Correctional Association (1990b and 1998) has implemented several standards. Listed next are some standards that pertain to this concern.

> *Use of Force* (3-4198): Written policy, procedure, and practice restrict the use of physical force to instances of justifiable self-defense, protection of others, protection of property, and prevention of escapes, and then only as a last resort and in accordance with appropriate statutory authority. In no event is physical force justifiable as punishment. A written report is prepared following all uses of force and is submitted to administrative staff for review.

> *Inmate Count* (3-4101): The institution maintains a daily report on inmate population movement.

> *Perimeter Security* (3-4164): The institution's perimeter is controlled by appropriate means to provide that inmates remain within the perimeter and to prevent access by the general public without proper authorization.

> *Emergency Plans* (3-4208): All institution personnel are trained in the implementation of written emergency plans. Work stoppage and disturbance or riot plans are communicated only to appropriate supervisory or other personnel directly involved in the implementation of those plans.

Gangs and Other Special Groups

Another factor in the organization of inmate population is the emergence of inmate gangs, also known as "security threat groups" (Miller and Rush, 1996). Populations in long-term facilities and in some jails tend to organize themselves by similarities. The four most common areas by which inmates group themselves are race, previous street gang membership, religious affiliation, and geographical predisposition. The more similar the inmates are in background, the greater the likelihood that they will be able to come together as one and react against the institution.

Gang membership is attractive to many inmates. It provides a sense of identity and belonging in a place where many other support systems (career, family, and neighborhood) have been stripped away. Gangs may provide inmates with a sense of protection, and this can be an initial motivating factor for an inmate to join such a group. At classification, gang members are asked to identify their gang affiliations so they will not be sent to a facility or housed in a cell with a rival gang (Glick, Sturgeon, Venator-Santiago, 1998).

Central Correctional Institution, Columbia, South Carolina. (*Source:* South Carolina State Archives)

Violent street gangs, as well as prison-generated gangs, have become a major dilemma for prison administrators. During the time individuals are subjected to the prison environment, they often continue such affiliations as a tool of survival. Miller and Rush (1996) estimate that between 80 and 90 percent of the inmates in many prison systems have some affiliation with street gangs. These individuals often come into the system with extensive histories in the criminal justice system. The groups have demonstrated a tendency to be violent, organized, and sophisticated enough to control resources (drugs, gambling, contraband, and so forth). If possible, such gangs will influence every aspect of prison life.

Many of the past prison riots in western states were attributed to racial conflict between inmate gangs. For example, in California, the four major prison gangs in the 1970s and 1980s were the Aryan Brotherhood, the Black Guerrilla Family, Nuestra Familia, and the Mexican Mafia (Miller and Rush, 1996). These gangs engaged in narcotics trafficking, pressuring and physically coercing inmates, and promulgating revolutionary political doctrines.

On October 18, 1981, a disturbance took place at the Nevada State Prison. It erupted when the Black Warrior Gang tried to stop prison authorities from locking two of their members in maximum-security housing. The disturbance lasted three hours and resulted in no property damage. Three correctional officers were stabbed and beaten. Force was used to end the disturbance.

On October 25, 1986, a battle between 200 prisoners—about 100 blacks and 100 whites—erupted in the Arizona State Prison. This prison was known as a stronghold for the Aryan Brotherhood (a white supremacist gang). Inmates battled with home-made knives, steel pipes, and baseball bats on an athletic field. Gangs of white and black prisoners began fighting minutes after a black inmate was stabbed and critically wounded in retaliation for the murder of a white convict the previous day. Order was restored within thirty minutes when twenty-six guards fired shotgun blasts and tear gas over the prisoners' heads.

On April 21, 1993, a riot took place at Garner Correctional Institution in Newtown, Connecticut. The triggering cause was a fight between gang members from the Latin Kings, Solidos Nation, and Brotherhood against members of the 20 Love gang. Eventually, a total of seventy-one inmates became involved in this seven-hour riot, which caused $150,000 in property damages. Nineteen staff were injured. The riot ended when inmates were told that the Correctional Emergency Response Team (CERT) was prepared to use force. Inmates voluntarily locked themselves in their cells.

A disturbance took place at the U.S. Penitentiary at Leavenworth, Kansas, on June 21, 1993. It was triggered when five members of the Mexican Mafia attacked and mortally wounded the local leader of the Texas Syndicate. This attack occurred in the recreation yard. Additional altercations began to take place between inmates who had homemade weapons. No staff were injured; however, one inmate was killed and six others were wounded. Four inmates required medical attention at a local hospital. The property damage was not significant. However, costs were approximately $600,000 for medical services, staff overtime, and additional food services required as a result of the riot. The staff that responded to the incident had to be fed and food service at the institution was interrupted. The disturbance ended within thirty minutes when two tower officers fired eight warning shots. Other staff were successful at separating the inmates involved and closing the recreation yard.

On January 19, 1994, a disturbance took place at the U.S. Penitentiary at Terre Haute, Indiana. It was triggered when a group of black inmates from California (mostly Bloods and Crips) attacked black Washington, D. C. inmates in the dining room. The attacking inmates were armed with homemade weapons. The disturbance lasted thirty minutes and involved fifty-six inmates. No hostages were taken in this disturbance, which resulted in injuries to four staff. Two inmates were injured; one was seriously injured from a stab wound. The cost, including overtime, amounted to $227,000. The distur-bance ended when the inmates who had been attacked left the area. The staff succeeded in apprehending the attackers.

Figure 2.5. Further Examples of Riots Caused by Gangs

Date	Institution	Consequences
Dec. 26, 1983	Youthful Offender Unit (GA)	65 inmates involved Lasted 30 minutes
Sept. 13, 1991	USP-Leavenworth (KS)	10 inmates involved
July, 1992	Maximum Unit (RI)	100 inmates involved $50,000 in damages "5%ers gang" assaulted staff
July 12, 1994	Robinson Correctional Institution (CT)	300 inmates involved $303,420 in damages 2 inmates killed
July 23, 1995	Allendale Correctional Institution (SC)	200 inmates involved 3 inmates injured

Analysis of Gangs and Other Special Groups

If prison administrators do not have clear control of their facilities, prison gangs will attempt to exert their influence over other inmates and correctional staff. To supervise the activities of any inmate group properly, particularly a gang, correctional staff must know a great deal about who they are. Maintaining strong relationships with local law enforcement from the areas where these inmates come from will allow intelligence-sharing that may assist in the identification of possible gang leaders who are entering a particular institution. On admission to the system, correctional staff can gain significant gang intelligence during the reception and evaluation process (Miller and Rush, 1996).

There are several other gang-control strategies, including separating gang members (sometimes known as "bus therapy"). By transferring members to different institutions, facility administrators can decrease the gang's hold on a particular institution. Such a strategy often is targeted at segregating inmate gang leaders. The access denied to these leaders makes it much more difficult for them to maintain a proper level of control over their groups. This separating process also can apply to the separation of rival gangs to decrease the tension within an institution.

Placing a facility on "lockdown" status because of gang problems or for other reasons also can prove to be an effective strategy for controlling an institution on the verge of rioting. While this is only a temporary solution, it provides the time needed for prison officials to identify and react to the situation at hand.

Controlling inmate gangs must be understood within the larger context of managing an entire prison system. Formally stated rules of conduct must be consistently and fairly applied to the inmate population. These rules, of course, must include prohibitions against gang-related activities. These training programs often serve as an appropriate response to gang-related activities. When institutional facilitators interact fairly, equally,

> Any new person, they hollered obscenities at them and all sorts of names, and throwing things down from the gallery and everything. They told me to walk down the middle of this line like I was on exhibition, and everybody started to throw things and everything, and I was shaking in my boots. . . . They were screaming things like, "That is for me," and "Look at his eyes," and "her eyes" or whatever, and making all kinds of remarks (Hans Toch, 1977).

and consistently with the inmates, there is less incentive for individuals to join gangs. Following are some American Correctional Association (1980 and 1998) standards to help reduce gang violence in correctional institutions.

Admissions (3-4273): Written policy, procedure, and practice require the preparation of a summary admission report for all new admissions. The report includes at a minimum the following information: legal aspects of the case, summary of criminal history, social history, medical-dental-mental health history, occupational experience and interests, educational status and interests, vocational programming, recreational preference and needs assessment, psychological evaluation, staff recommendations, and preinstitutional assessment information.

Sharing of Information (3-4099): The institution or parent agency collaborates with criminal justice and service agencies in information gathering, exchange, and standardization.

Inmate Movement (3-4181): Written policy, procedure, and practice provide that staff regulate inmate movement.

Segregation (3-4238): The warden/superintendent or shift supervisor can order immediate segregation when it is necessary to protect the inmate or others. The action is reviewed within seventy-two hours by the appropriate authority.

Rumors

A prison riot can be triggered merely by rumors. The truthfulness of the rumor is not important, it is the perception of the rumor by the inmates who hear it. These rumors usually are one of two types. The first type consists of rumors based on the unequal (special) treatment of inmates, while the second type are rumors of mistreatment of other inmates by the administration (such as inmates assaulted by correctional officers). Rumors often result from inconsistent enforcement of rules by correctional staff or unclear rules. Such inconsistencies in enforcement tend to generate higher levels of disbelief within an institutional setting. This induces a lack of trust of the administration and the policies they impose.

For example, on November 24, 1964, a prison riot took place at the Maryland House of Corrections (Jessup, Maryland). The reported cause was a rumor that an inmate had been beaten after he was locked in a security cell. This riot lasted three hours and involved 800 inmates, two of whom were injured.

On August 9, 1969, a disturbance took place at the Allegheny County Prison in Pittsburgh, Pennsylvania. The triggering event was a rumor that correctional officers had abused an inmate. The disturbance lasted twenty minutes and resulted in injuries to two correctional officers.

On November 12, 1971, a disturbance took place at the Green Bay Reformatory in Wisconsin. The triggering cause was a rumor that correctional officers were beating some inmates. The disturbance involved over 200 inmates but lasted only thirty minutes. One inmate and five correctional officers were injured.

The Fountain Correctional Center in Atmore, Alabama, experienced a prison riot on January 18, 1974. The rumor, which triggered the riot, was that a black inmate at a nearby correctional facility had died as a result of force used by correctional officers. The inmates involved in "Inmates for Action" (IFA), a black militant group, began rioting. The uprising lasted two hours and resulted in $2,000 of damages to windows, furniture, and fixtures. One correctional officer and one inmate were killed in the riot. The riot ended when correctional officers, state troopers, sheriff's deputies, and local police entered the prison in force, armed with shotguns, and restored order.

On September 30, 1991, a riot erupted on the prison yard of the Maximum Security Facility in Rhode Island (Cranston, Rhode Island). Rumors among inmates suggested that two new deputy wardens would change their living conditions. This five-hour riot involved 293 inmates and resulted in $1.4 million dollars worth of damages. All inmates voluntarily agreed to return to their cells after presenting a list of demands to prison officials. One of the demands mandated that the previous deputy warden be returned to his post. The administration agreed to discuss the demands at a later date but made no commitments or guarantees.

Figure 2.6. Additional Examples of Riots Caused by Rumors

Date	Institution	Consequences
Aug. 22, 1954	North Carolina Women's Prison (NC)	300 inmates involved Rumor of the death of an 18-year-old in an isolation cell
Oct. 27, 1954	Missouri Women's Prison (MO)	Rumor concerning the attention men received in a 10/23/54 riot
Mar. 30, 1960	Stafford County Jail (NH)	Rumors of a guard slaying inmate in another jail
Aug. 13, 1963	Indiana State Penal Farm (IN)	1,400 inmates involved Lasted 90 minutes Rumor that an 18-year-old inmate had died because of inadequate medical treatment
June 13, 1983	Perry Correctional Institution (SC)	Lasted 4 hours 2 hostages taken Thought an inmate had been beaten by a security guard

Analysis of Rumors

It is not surprising that inconsistent policy enforcement may result in varied treatment of inmates. This "different" treatment can lead to the generation of rumors, which then can lead to fights and arguments between inmates, as well as between inmates and staff. The failure to apply rules in a fair, firm, and consistent, way can trigger a violent outbreak. To combat this, both staff and inmates must recognize the rules and the uniform penalty for violations, as well as create an awareness that the rules will be enforced.

Another strong influence that helps to determine the security level of an institution is the quality of communication. This includes communication exchanges between administration, staff, and inmates. Correctional officers continually need to be informed about new policies, procedures, and inmate programs. Inmates often are misinformed about changes in policies and procedures that affect them; thus, rumors and misinformation will spread. These rumors eventually may result in a riot or disturbance. Therefore, inmates should be informed clearly and repeatedly when a change occurs that affects them. Also, correctional staff must be sure to dispel rumors and replace misinformation with accurate facts. Following such practices with a high level of consistency will generate trust and safety between the inmates and the institution (American Correctional Association, 1990a).

Perhaps one of the most useful strategies that administrators can employ to avoid institutional violence is that of "roving management." This philosophy requires that the warden spend time moving throughout the institution and talking with inmates in an informal manner. Studies have revealed that 15 percent more wardens in "nonrioting" prisons reported spending twenty-six hours or more per month in direct contact with inmates than wardens in "riot" prisons. Additionally, about 13 percent more wardens in "riot" prisons spent fifteen hours or less per month in contact with inmates than wardens in "nonrioting" prisons (American Correctional Association, 1990a). In survey after survey, inmates have expressed their discontent when their opinions and problems do not reach the top decision-making post. The American Correctional Association (1990b and 1998) has created standards to be followed throughout correctional institutions to reduce the incidence of rumors that may escalate to the level of a disturbance or riot.

> *Rules of Conduct* (3-4216): A rulebook that contains all chargeable offenses, ranges of penalties, and disciplinary procedures is given to each inmate and staff member and is translated into those languages spoken by significant numbers of inmates. Signed acknowledgment of receipt of the rulebook is maintained in the inmate's file. When a literacy or language problem prevents an inmate from understanding the rulebook, a staff member or translator assists the inmate in understanding the rules.

> *Channels of Communication* (3-4016): Written policy, procedure, and practice provide for regular meetings between the warden/superintendent and all department heads and between department heads and their key staff members. Such meetings are to be conducted at least monthly.

> *Two-way Communication* (3-4017): Written policy, procedure, and practice provide for a system of two-way communication between all levels of staff and inmates.

Security Issues

Perhaps the most overriding element that allows disturbances and riots to develop is the attitude that staff may have about security. In many investigations conducted after a riot has occurred, officials learn that inmates had acquired facility schematics, institutional emergency plans, keys, electrical diagrams, weapons, food supplies, and staff

Weapons and tools found at Kirkland Correctional Institution, Columbia, South Carolina.
(*Source:* South Carolina Department of Corrections – Mr. Al Waters' Collection)

clothing. Yet, the most important duty of correctional personnel is to maintain security and prevent these things from happening (*See* Henderson, Rauch, and Phillips, 1997)

On March 7, 1973, a prison riot was recorded for the Idaho State Penitentiary (Boise, Idaho). Approximately forty inmates became involved in this riot. The riot was triggered when an inmate was taken from x-ray back to the maximum-security unit. Other inmates blocked this process. Some inmates also began setting fires. The riot lasted four hours and caused $100,000 worth of damages. The tactical unit used force to regain control and end the riot.

Unit number 25 (Botetourt Correctional Unit 25 in Troutville, Virginia) experienced a riot in 1975 when a power outage caused a breakdown in security. Thirty inmates rioted for three hours and caused $5,000 worth of damages. No injuries were reported, and the situation ended by a show of force and extensively lighting the facility.

On July 23, 1980, a riot took place at the Idaho State Correctional Institution (a facility that replaced the Idaho State Penitentiary). This riot was triggered by an evacuation of living units to clear out large buildups of contraband. Approximately 200 inmates were involved in this riot. Two correctional officers were taken hostage. No staff were injured, but seventeen inmates received minor injuries. This nineteen-hour riot caused $2.3 million dollars worth of damages. The riot lasted one day, and was ended by negotiation.

The West Virginia State Penitentiary (Moundsville, West Virginia) had a prison riot on January 1, 1986. The riot ended after forty-two hours of inmate control. This old institution was designed for 696 inmates, but 741 inmates were held there the day of the riot. This institution had a history of loose security, many locks to cells did not work, and contraband was not controlled. Staff pay and morale was also low. A major cause of the riot was a prison crackdown on security after an inmate escaped and killed a police officer. A new warden imposed strong rules governing visitation; inmates could not receive packages from former inmates; and inmates were ordered to reduce the amount of property in their cells.

Inmates on death row in the Indiana State Prison (Michigan City, Indiana) rioted on March 17, 1986. The fourteen inmates did not like security measures and the double celling. The riot lasted twelve and a half hours and resulted in a minor injury to one staff member. There was no property damage, and the riot ended as a result of negotiations.

On April 1, 1986, there was a prison riot at the Kirkland Correctional Institution in Columbia, South Carolina, which held 951 men. This riot is also known as the April Fool's Day Riot. The four-hour riot started when an inmate requested that a correctional officer bring him some Tylenol. As the officer entered the unit to deliver the medication, he was approached from behind by an inmate holding a sixteen-inch homemade knife. The inmate threatened the officer if he did not turn over his keys. The officer put the keys on the concrete floor, and ran from the scene to notify other correctional officers, who sounded the prison alarm. In a matter of minutes, thirty-two inmates had been released from their high-security cells. These inmates freed other inmates in the unit, who moved into the yard.

Inmates climbed over the unit D recreation yard fence and broke open a large tool box. The box held crowbars, metal side grinders, bolt cutters, power saws, sledge hammers, and acetylene cutting equipment. These tools previously had been used for renovation work in the unit. Inmates in the general population dorms were freed by the rioting inmates. A total of twenty-two employees were taken hostage or were trapped in their buildings. Some employees were hidden by inmates in their cells. Two correctional officers were beaten by inmates.

The treatment building, education building, library, and administrative offices in the dorms were set on fire. Inmates only were able to take control of half of the institution, due to the quick thinking of one correctional officer, who had positioned himself on the roof of the administration building. He fired a warning shot with a 12 gauge shotgun over the heads of inmates who were trying to reach the main administration building, the infirmary, the cafeteria, the prison industries building, and the Gilliam Psychiatric Center. This blast caused the inmates to run back to their dorms.

A correctional officer, who was trapped with ten other officers, telephoned the command post in the warden's office. He stated that inmates were trying to break into their space. The inmates were armed with a cutting torch and numerous weapons. The Commissioner of Corrections decided that immediate action by the three emergency response teams was necessary. The warden made an announcement over the public address system instructing inmates to lie on the ground. He also informed them that a riot squad armed with shotguns had been deployed to end the riot.

The thirty-five members of the Reserve Emergency Platoon regained control of unit D and freed the hostages, who were brought to the conference room in the administration building for debriefing. Emergency teams then were ordered to route inmates to the recreation field and contain them at that location. Each building was searched for remaining hostages or inmates.

The warden made a second announcement instructing nonparticipating inmates to report to the recreation field (Catoe and Harvey, 1986). While the warden was speaking, forty members of the emergency teams moved 600 inmates into the fenced area. Another 100 inmates were moved into the unit D fenced recreation yard; 100 more were found locked in their rooms. The entire institution was finally under control and all buildings were secured. Inmates were frisk-searched and moved to their assigned dorms.

Over the next several days, the inmates who were directly involved in the riot were moved from Kirkland to Central Correctional Institution in the center of Columbia, South Carolina. A formal debriefing was held April 7 for all employees who had been held as hostages. This group session allowed employees to express their feelings in the hope of reducing tensions. Total smoke and fire damage to the Kirkland Correctional Institution totaled $732,000. The Grand Jury for Richland County returned thirty-six indictments against twenty-five inmates for rioting, inciting to riot, and/or taking hostages.

The major lessons learned from the Kirkland riot are the following: (1) security in units with violent inmates needs to be checked on a continuous basis to prevent assaults on officers, (2) emergency response teams should be deployed as soon as possible after a riot begins, (3) rioting should be contained as much as possible, and prevented from moving to different units in a correctional facility, (4) rioting inmates should be told that maximum force will be used, if necessary, to restore order to the institution, (5) correctional officers need debriefing sessions after a riot to reduce personal stress, and (6) prosecution of inmates who take part in a riot is essential to demonstrate to others that destructive behavior will not be tolerated.

Washington State reported a prison riot for the Intensive Management Unit (IMU) of the Clallam Bay Correctional Center (Clallam Bay, Washington) on April 1, 1992. The reported cause was general disruption of the unit. Fifteen inmates were involved in this riot, which lasted forty-six hours. The destruction of cell windows was the major source of property damage. Officials used cell extraction to place inmates in stripped cells, thus ending the riot.

The riot started in the mess hall around 5:30 PM when correctional officers were attacked by inmates. Seventeen staff were taken hostage. A significant demand of the inmates was the appointment of a new warden. The inmates had fourteen additional demands, which ranged from better food preparation to an improved heating system to combat the cold West Virginia weather.

The Governor agreed to meet with inmate leaders in exchange for the release of the hostages and the return of the facility. A unique request of the inmates was the provision that they be allowed to clean the facility before returning the institution to prison officials. The riot ended in a peaceful manner; however, twenty-three inmates later were indicted.

Figure 2.7. Additional Examples of Riots Caused by Security Issues

Date	Institution	Consequences
May 25, 1975	Iowa State Penitentiary (IA)	1 hostage taken $10,000 in damages State patrol was called in
Jan. 20, 1989	Central Facility (VA)	Lasted 7 hours 1 inmate was killed
Dec. 4, 1991	Bayside State Prison (NJ)	$485 in damage Began during a transfer procedure
Dec. 8, 1991	Federal Correctional Institution (CA)	55 inmates participated
Aug. 12, 1993	Central Utah Correctional Facility (UT)	15 inmates involved $32,405 in damages Riot resulted from shakedown

Analysis of Security Issues

In almost any research study examining prison riots, there is consistently a positive association between the security classification of the prison and the occurrence of a riot. Of the riots reported by wardens and reviewed in this book, nearly 60 percent took place in maximum-security prisons. However, maximum-security institutions generally are densely populated; the term "maximum-security" may refer only to the design of the building, not necessarily to the social separation of inmates.

There is also a strong correlation between buildings and riots. There is a positive association between the planned capacity of a prison and its history of riots—the larger the prison's planned capacity, the greater the probability of a riot. There is also a positive association between the age of a prison and its history of riots: Older facilities demonstrate a higher occurrence of riots. The American Correctional Association (1990b and 1998) has created standards; some relate to maintaining effective security.

Threats to Security (3-4212): There are written plans that specify the procedures to be followed in situations that threaten institutional security. Such situations include but are not limited to riots, hunger strikes, disturbances, and taking of hostages. These plans are made available to all applicable personnel and are reviewed at least annually and updated as needed.

Evacuation Procedures (3-4210): Written policy, procedure, and practice specify the means for the immediate release of inmates from locked areas in case of emergency and provide for a backup system.

Patrols (3-4177): Written policy, procedure, and practice provide that supervisory staff conduct a daily patrol, including holidays and weekends, of all areas occupied by inmates and submit a daily written report to their supervisor. Unoccupied areas are to be inspected weekly.

Inspections (3-4179): Written policy, procedure, and practice require that the chief security officer or qualified designee conduct at least weekly inspections of all security devices needing repair or maintenance and report the results of the inspections in writing.

Inmate Counts (3-4180): The institution has a system for physically counting inmates. The system includes strict accountability for inmates assigned to work and educational release, furloughs, and other approved temporary absences.

Conflict with Other Inmates

In correctional facilities, inmates are forced to associate with others who have histories of aggressive, violent behavior. Because of the heightened level of violence, many inmates feel the need to fight for their safety and possessions. If inmates compromise their position, they risk humiliation and exploitation. Thus, any loss of security can be extremely frightening. A prison riot can result from conflicts between inmates.

> Severe injuries resulted when two inmates in a federal prison got into a fight. This incident was observed by a correctional officer who choose to contain the fight by locking the section where the inmates were fighting, rather than choosing to intervene. The Supreme Court ruled that it was just for the injured inmate (who had suffered a fractured skull) to bring suit (Federal Tort Claims Act of 1946) against the federal government, including its employees, for negligence. *United States v. Muniz*, 374 U.S. 150, 83 S.Ct. 1850 (1963).

Each area of a facility (cafeteria, dormitory, recreation area, and so forth) has its own innate characteristics that may indicate the potential for an impending riot. Other variables indicating a potential riot include separation by racial or ethnic groups, a group member facing away from their group, inmate violence against other inmates, appearance of inflammatory and rebellious materials, and increasing numbers of complaints and grievances. For example, on December 1, 1952, a disturbance exploded after two inmates began fighting in the Sheridan State Reformatory in Sheridan, Illinois. This disturbance lasted 30 minutes and involved 100 inmates.

On April 28, 1982, an inmate dispute erupted into a disturbance at the Zephyr Hills Correctional Institution in Zephyr Hills, Florida. This disturbance involved fifteen inmates and resulted in injuries to one inmate and two correctional officers. Damages included forty broken windows and two stolen canteens with $750 cash. The disturbance lasted forty minutes and ended as a result of voluntary surrender.

On October 27, 1984, a disturbance erupted at the Federal Correctional Institution in Englewood, Colorado. Fifty inmates took part in this disturbance, which started when inmates from one living unit attacked inmates of another unit. A total of nineteen inmates were injured, but there were only minor damages to the living unit.

A disturbance took place at the Federal Prison in Lompoc, California on August 25, 1989. Two groups of black inmates, one from Los Angeles and the other from the District of Columbia, had a dispute over an illicit-drug transaction. Approximately fifty inmates were involved in this disturbance, which lasted thirty minutes. There was no property damage but four inmates were injured. The two groups were armed with baseball bats and weight bars. The riot ended when one group managed to flee, and staff were able to close the recreation yard behind them.

On June 15, 1992, a riot occurred at the Federal Correctional Institution in Big Spring, Texas. This riot, which eventually involved 300, began as a fight between 3 black and 3 Hispanic inmates. This fighting escalated into a confrontation between black and Hispanic inmates. Many were armed with weapons, such as broom handles and metal rods torn from chairs. Two staff members received minor injuries, and one inmate suffered a serious blow to the face. No serious property damage was reported. The riot lasted six and a half hours and ended when additional staff were called to increase security and help separate the hostile groups of inmates. A funnel cloud was sighted near the institution, further encouraging ending of the riot. Tornado sirens finally convinced inmates to return to their living units.

Clallam Bay Correctional Center in Washington State had a disturbance in D unit on September 1, 1992. The reported cause was a fight between two inmates. The disturbance involved fifteen inmates and lasted three hours. Four staff and one inmate received minor injuries. A show of force ended the disturbance, which caused only $100 worth of damages to property.

The same institution reported a riot for April 15, 1995, in the A unit. This two-and-a-half-hour riot involved fifteen inmates. It began with two inmates fighting and generally causing trouble. Approximately $35,000 worth of damage to windows, locks, doors, and the sprinkler system was reported. The inmates surrendered after explosive diversionary devices were used and the CERT team entered the unit. (Note: the analysis of conflicts with other inmates is discussed on pages 40-42.)

Figure 2.8. Further Examples of Riots Caused by Conflicts with Other Inmates

Date	Institution	Consequences
Oct. 4, 1971	Pontiac State Penitentiary (IL)	Lasted 4 hours $65,000 in damages
Mar. 10, 1992	Bridgeport (CT)	100 inmates involved $3,042 in damages
Aug. 16, 1992	Potosi Correctional Center (MO)	100 inmates involved
May 3, 1993	Morrison (NC)	50 inmates involved
Jan. 10, 1993	Multi-Purpose Criminal Justice Facility (DE)	20 inmates involved

Conflict with Correctional Staff

A riot or disturbance can result from conflicts between correctional staff and inmates. For example, on October 1, 1969, a disturbance took place at the Wisconsin State Reformatory (Green Bay Correctional Institution, Green Bay, Wisconsin) after a confrontation between a correctional officer and inmates. Seventy inmates were involved; one correctional officer and one civilian were injured. The disturbance ended when the security captain listened to inmate complaints and persuaded them to return to their cells.

On July 5, 1970, a disturbance took place at the Holmesburg State Prison, in Philadelphia, Pennsylvania. The triggering cause was the attack on a correctional officer by an inmate. Official reports do not establish the cause of the attack. Six hostages were held by the rioting inmates. Eighty inmates and six correctional officers were injured.

During the month of August, 1980, a prison riot erupted at the Halawa High Security Facility in Hawaii. The triggering cause was a disagreement between a staff member and an inmate. Fifty inmates joined the fight, and caused $318,000 in property damages. Injuries included scratches and bruises to inmates and correctional officers. The riot ended after three hours, by the use of force.

On August 26, 1980, a disturbance took place at the Union Correctional Institution in Raiford, Florida. An inmate assault on a correctional officer triggered this uprising. Two hundred inmates became involved in the activity, which lasted thirty-five minutes. Three correctional officers were injured. The disturbance ended by means of voluntary surrender.

On November 4, 1981, a riot occurred at the Somers Correctional Institution in Somers, Connecticut. The triggering cause was the belief of inmates that a correctional officer had taken abusive action against a Hispanic inmate. A group of about forty inmates took over the gym area. Nine staff members were injured, and one was taken hostage. The institutional property damage amounted to $14,000. The hostage was released unharmed after five hours. The inmates voluntarily surrendered.

The South Dakota Penitentiary at Sioux Falls reported a disturbance for November 7, 1981. This uprising resulted from a fight between three correctional officers and four inmates who refused to return to their cells. At this point, other inmates joined in the fight by brandishing broom handles and homemade knives. A total of twenty inmates were involved in the disturbance, which resulted in ten injuries to correctional staff. Officers using force finally were able to regain control of the cell block.

The federal prison system reported a riot at the Lewisburg, Pennsylvania prison on July 10, 1992. The reported cause was the refusal of inmates to return to their assigned cubicles for the midnight count. Instead, the inmates armed themselves. One lieutenant received a severe blow to his forearm and five staff received burns from a stingball grenade. Thirty-one inmates had injuries ranging from minor wounds to lacerations. The riot was ended when the SORT team secured half of the unit using stingball grenades and stun munitions. The other half of the unit was regained with additional stingball grenades.

Figure 2.9. Further Examples of Riots Caused by Conflicts with Correctional Staff

Date	Institution	Consequences
Sept. 23, 1991	Nebraska Center for Women (NE)	Refused to return to rooms, Forcibly taken to segregation
Sept. 30, 1991	Maximum Facility (RI)	293 inmates involved $1,000,000 in damages Leveled a greenhouse
Apr., 28, 1992	Smithfield (PA)	10 inmates involved
Nov. 25, 1992	Enfield Correctional Institution (CT)	400 inmates involved $140,000 in damages
May 22, 1993	LCF (KS)	Lasted 30 minutes Attack on officers

Analysis of Conflicts with Correctional Staff and Other Inmates

Several signs illustrate the generation of tension. These range from (1) hostility or arguments among inmates, or between inmates and staff, (2) fights, (3) grievances and complaints, (4) unusual incidents as expressions of aggression and violence (such as unprovoked destruction of personal or institutional property), and (5) noise levels in the mess hall, yard, or recreation areas. Attention to the buildup or momentum of such single events will provide the observer with a greater understanding of the potential consequences.

Awareness of empirical evidence relating to prison violence also will serve as a strong ally in maintaining positive control of a correctional institution. Studies have shown that violence was more likely in institutional settings effected by chronic, long-term crowding and idleness. This level of potential violence also was shown to be directly modified by frequent changes in the institution's rules, regulations, and personnel.

There is a higher probability of prison violence when young prisoners with long sentences are involved (Braswell, Montgomery, and Lombardo, 1994, p. 255). These individuals have little to lose, and with this absence of "hope," they are typically much more predisposed to violent behavior. Another study stated that two identifiable inmate behaviors increased the disciplinary response levels of actions taken by correctional officers: (1) prisoners being verbally hostile to officers, and (2) prisoners refusing to follow orders.

To avoid these problems, certain strategies often are employed by institutional staff. Treating all inmates with an expected level of respect, while maintaining a high level of professionalism, is the most important course of action. This strategy has been advocated by the American Correctional Association which has stated that for optimal results, correctional officers should treat inmates fairly, firmly, consistently, and equally (American Correctional Association, 1996b, p. 114).

Another strategy to prevent riots is the establishment and maintenance of open lines of communication between inmates and institutional staff. These strategies are ultimately important in affecting the emotional climate of an institution because correctional officers and work supervisors have the most contact with inmates. Therefore, their knowledge and competence are of utmost importance in maintaining the day-to-day flow of information in an institution. A major concern of officers is generally the legal liabilities they may incur. To protect correctional officers whenever a physical confrontation is anticipated (such as forced cell moves), the action should be videotaped. This objective and technological witness may prove to be the last and best line of legal self-defense for both the officer and the correctional institution involved.

Another issue that must be addressed concerning correctional staff includes that of adequate training. A national survey found that correctional officers said they needed more training (37.9 percent of those surveyed) on how to respond to incidents requiring force. Thirty-one percent wanted improved corrections technology, more use-of-force technology (28.8 percent), additional staff (25.4 percent), and more interpersonal-communications training (19.8 percent) (Henry, Senese, and Ingley, 1994). These concerns proved to be significant at both the infamous Attica and Santa Fe riots. The lack of training and preparation of the correctional officers for their positions was made a major issue in the charges following these riots. In both prisons, the officers were untrained in handling prison violence and were seldom trained in any way, other than "on the job," for all aspects of their work.

In addition, the first-line supervisor must be committed to doing his or her best with respect to leading the other officers. Insisting on excellence from subordinate staff is not unreasonable if the supervisor and the institution maintain the same level of personal commitment (Billy, 1996).

With these factors in mind, institutional administrators must remember the importance of staff training and familiarity with the rules and regulations, as well as the value of briefing employees on changes that may be forthcoming immediately. Of course, like any well-run business, good communication starts at the top, and the results are a well-informed staff that can cohesively implement organizational change (American Correctional Association, 1996b).

ACA standards (1990b and 1998) related to these issues include the following:

- *Rated Capacity* (3-4126): The number of inmates does not exceed the facility's rated bed capacity.

- *Noise Levels* (3-4143): Noise levels in inmate housing units do not exceed 70dBA in daytime and 45dBA at night.

- *Staff/Inmate Interaction* (3-4122): Physical plant design facilitates personal contact and interaction between staff and inmates.

- *Facility Size* (3-4123): Institutions of more than 500 inmates are divided into distinct, semiautonomous management units that encourage positive staff and inmate interactions. Staff within each management unit are delegated the authority to make decisions regarding security classification, services, and programs for inmates within the unit.

- *Resolution of Minor Infractions* (3-4218): There are written guidelines for resolving minor inmate infractions, which include a written statement of the rule violated and a hearing and decision within seven days, excluding weekends and holidays, by a person not involved in the rule violation; the inmate may waive the hearing.

- *Protection from Harm* (3-4268): Written policy, procedure, and practice protect inmates from personal abuse, corporal punishment, personal injury, disease, property damage, and harassment.

Alcohol and Other Drug Usage

An underlying factor in some prison riots is the use of alcohol and other drugs. For example, on November 14, 1964, a disturbance was reported for the State Vocational School for Girls in Montana. It involved twenty inmates who had became intoxicated on fingernail polish remover fumes.

On August 13, 1966, a disturbance occurred at the Walpole State Prison (Massachusetts Correctional Institution - Cedar Junction) in Walpole, Massachusetts. Fifteen inmates were involved in this disturbance, where the reported cause was the attempted theft of drugs. Nine inmates were injured in this uprising, which lasted two hours.

A disturbance between inmates and correctional officers occurred at the Central Correctional Institution, Columbia, South Carolina, on April 1, 1968. An article in *The State* (McCuen, 1968) newspaper the following day described this event in detail. The article stated:

> Warden J. W. Strickland said two inmates jumped two guards as the officers were placing another inmate in his cell on suspicion of being drunk. Officials say he had apparently concocted a home brew. He said two guards were injured in this struggle when they were struck with a club. Only one guard was hospitalized.

> Strickland said the two attacking inmates then ran down the prison's main corridor to the cafeteria and began overturning tables and chairs. One of the two inmates then ran out into the corridor where guards attempted to arrest him. Some 75 inmates gathered there and part of a small tear gas canister was used to break up the crowd. He said several inmates ran out into the prison yard, where they smashed windows in a vocational rehabilitation building and a guard station. Others ran down the prison corridor and smashed four windows in a guard station. A core of only about 15 inmates were actually involved in this. We have arrested seven inmates and have placed them in security pending charges. We have not yet confiscated any weapons, but an investigation is continuing, said Strickland.

> MacDougall, the Director, said the entire disturbance lasted about an hour. He said two units of riot-trained correctional officers were ordered to stand by, but it was not necessary to use them.

On January 2, 1973, a disturbance took place at the Utah State Prison in Draper City. Approximately fifteen inmates were involved in the event. Inmates, drunk on home-made brew, began throwing cans, bottles, and televisions from the top tiers. They set fire in one of the cells.

A riot took place at the Washington State Penitentiary in Walla Walla on December 30, 1974. Sixty inmates took part in this riot, which was initiated to take over the hospital's drug supply. This riot lasted for twenty-five hours.

On June 27, 1980, a disturbance erupted at the Oregon State Penitentiary in Salem. Intoxicated inmates were being transported to segregation when they resisted. A security manager was taken hostage with a knife at his throat. Fourteen inmates destroyed $2,000 worth of property and beat other inmates. The disturbance lasted over one hour. Control was restored when prison officials stormed the rioters. A peaceful three-day lockdown followed the disturbance.

The Centennial Correctional Facility in Canon City, Colorado was the setting for a disturbance on October 11, 1982. The triggering cause was the use of homemade brew by approximately fifteen inmates. The rioting inmates destroyed $2,500 worth of property in the three-and-a-half-hour disturbance. The only physical injury occurred when an inmate was cut with broken glass. Force was used to end the disturbance.

On May 5, 1993, a prison riot took place at the South Dakota Penitentiary in Sioux Falls. The riot was triggered by intoxicated inmates in the yard. Two staff members were assaulted in the riot that resulted in approximately $1,339,400 worth of damages. Three inmates were prosecuted in state court for their actions. Other inmates were disciplined by the Department of Corrections.

Figure 2.10. Further Examples of Riots Caused by Alcohol and Other Drugs

Date	Institution	Consequences
June, 1972	Indiana Reformatory (IN)	100 inmates involved Drunk on homemade brew Lasted 2 hours
Aug. 11, 1973	Central Correctional Institution (SC)	100 inmates involved 1 officer hospitalized
Mar. 18, 1974	Kentucky Correctional Institution for Women (KY)	40 inmates involved Lasted 40 minutes
Nov. 3, 1982	Southeast Brunswick Correctional Center (VA)	175 inmates involved Lasted 2 days $8,000 in damages

Analysis of Alcohol and Other Drug Usage

The problems raised in a correctional setting can become very complex when drugs and alcohol are involved; therefore, an institution must have standing prevention policies. Such efforts may be improved by considering the following recommendations:

- Unannounced and irregularly timed searches of cells, inmates, and inmate work areas

- Inspection of all vehicular traffic and supplies coming into the institution

- Use of metal detectors at compound gates and entrances into housing units

- Complete search and inspection of each cell prior to occupancy by a new inmate

- Avoidance of unnecessary force, embarrassment, or indignity to the inmate

- Staff training in effective search techniques that protect both inmates and staff from bodily harm

- Use of nonintensive sensors and other techniques instead of body searches, whenever feasible

> An Illinois inmate named Hughes was accused of consuming some liquor manufactured on penitentiary grounds (hooch). This was a violation of institutional rules; therefore, Hughes was placed in administrative segregation. Hughes brought suit, stating that his civil rights had been violated because he had not been given a hearing before his punishment was carried out. He had also been informed that he would be held responsible for the state's lawyer fees incurred during this incident (lawyers representing the attorney general).
>
> The Supreme Court held that because no emergency had been present to warrant the need for isolation (security issues), and no hearing had taken place, the resultant assignment of attorney fees was inappropriate. This case provided that inmates must be given a hearing prior to imposing punishment (unless emergency/security circumstances are involved). *Hughes v. Rowe*, 449 U.S. 5, 101 S.Ct. 173 (1980).

- Searches performed only as necessary to control contraband or to recover missing or stolen property

- Respect of inmates' rights to authorized personal property

- Use of only those mechanical devices absolutely necessary for security purposes (Henderson, Rauch, and Phillips, 1997)

While security issues may be the foremost concern of the institutional staff, the health of the inmate also must be considered. America's contemporary "war on drugs" has stimulated a large population of recently incarcerated prisoners experiencing the effects of chemical dependency withdrawal. Immediate detoxification of an inmate is a common experience in today's prisons. These incidents pose a special risk (for psychotics, seizure-prone inmates, pregnant inmates, juveniles, and elderly inmates) and, therefore, must be handled through specialized procedures or programs.

Often, inmates experiencing chemical-dependency complications must be serviced through an institutionally based treatment program. Typically, such a program is run by a specially trained substance abuse counselor. Each inmate generally is given an individual diagnosis and treatment program to follow. To conserve resources, the correctional institution uses existing community resources whenever possible to achieve the goals of its addiction program. Experts in chemical dependency make the following recommendations for treating inmates.

- Use staff trained in drug and alcoholic treatment to design and supervise the program

- Train and use former addicts and recovered alcoholics to serve as employees or volunteers in these programs

- Coordinate with community substance abuse programs

- Motivate addicts to seek help

- Set realistic goals for the rehabilitation of inmates with substance-abuse problems

- Use a variety of approaches to provide flexibility to meet the varying needs of different addicts (American Correctional Association, 1990a, p. 131)

The American Correctional Association recognized the impact that the use of alcohol and other drugs has had on the issues affecting American correctional facilities, and in accordance with proper security policies it has developed several standards on this topic (1990b and 1998), including the following:

Control of Contraband (3-4184): Written policy, procedure, and practice provide for searches of facilities and inmates to control contraband and provide for its disposition. These policies are made available to staff and inmates; policies and procedures are reviewed at least annually and updated, if necessary.

Detoxification (3-4370): Written policy, procedure, and practice require that gradual detoxification from alcohol, opiates, hypnotics, other stimulants, and sedative hypnotic drugs is conducted under medical supervision when performed at the facility or is conducted in a hospital or community detoxification center.

Management of Chemical Dependency (3-4371): Written policy, procedure, and practice provide for the clinical management of chemically dependent inmates and include the following: a) a standardized diagnostic needs assessment administered to determine the extent of use, abuse, dependency, and/or codependency, b) a medical examination to determine medical needs and/or observational requirements, c) an individualized treatment plan developed and implemented by a multidisciplinary team, d) prerelease relapse-prevention education including risk managment, e) aftercare discharge plans shall include the inmate.

Substance Abuse Programs (3-4388): Written policy, procedure, and practice provide for substance abuse programs for inmates with drug and alcohol addiction problems.

No Identifiable Triggering Event

Many riots have no known causes. On October 4, 1929, a riot was reported for the Colorado State Penitentiary in Canon City. There was no reported cause for this two-day riot, which involved 150 inmates. Five inmates, three correctional officers, and four hostages were killed. The riot ended when the inmates depleted their ammunition supply.

A disturbance involving twenty inmates took place at the Denver County Jail in Colorado, on July 19, 1952. It had no reported cause.

On February 27, 1976, a disturbance erupted in the fieldhouse at the Indiana Reformatory (Pendleton Correctional Facility, Pendleton, Indiana). This disturbance, which had no known cause, involved ninety inmates. Several inmates were injured and equipment in the field house was damaged. The disturbance ended when an officer fired a shot into a wall. The inmates decided to surrender after this.

The San Francisco County Jail in California reported a riot for May 5, 1952. This riot involved 240 inmates and lasted twenty-four hours. There was no reported cause for this riot.

Another California facility in San Bruno reported a prison disturbance on October 25, 1954 without any reported cause. Four hundred inmates were involved in this disturbance, which lasted one hour.

The Federal Correctional Institution at Englewood, Colorado, experienced a disturbance, on November 2, 1993. There was no reported cause for this disturbance, which involved fifty inmates. The inmates broke windows and set fires in a dormitory living unit. No staff were injured; however, one inmate was treated for minor smoke inhalation. The SORT team and two disturbance control squads regained control of the living units. Inmates were removed from the units and transferred to other federal prisons.

Figure 2.11. Further Examples of Riots With No Known Cause

Date	Institution	Consequences
Dec. 12, 1929	Auburn Prison (NY)	50 inmates involved Lasted 6 hours 8 inmates and 1 officer killed
Nov. 25, 1947	Wisconsin State Prison (WI)	69 inmates involved 4 hostages taken Lasted 8 hours
Aug. 9, 1960	South Dakota State Penitentiary (SD)	50 inmates involved 4 officers injured Lasted 1 1/2 hours
Aug. 11, 1970	Tombs (NY)	800 inmates involved 3 hostages taken Lasted 7 hours
May 19, 1993	Varner Unit (AR)	40 inmates involved
Nov. 11, 1993	Somers (CT)	35 inmates involved $77,350 in damages

Analysis of "No Known Triggering Event"

The anticipation of an incident within a correctional setting, as this section's title implies, often is difficult to predict. However, in general, trained correctional staff should be aware of typical signs. According to the American Correctional Association (1996b), the capacity for trouble can be perceived as intensifying if there is an annual growth (or abrupt month-to-month growth) for general population inmates and disciplinary unit inmates in the number (or percentage) of actions listed in the following categories:

Long-term Statistical Indicators
- Inmate-on-staff assaults
- Inmate-on-inmate assaults
- Incidents of disruptive behavior
- Inmate-set fires
- Officers reporting minor, moderate, or serious injuries at the hands of inmates
- Reports of urine, feces, or food thrown at staff by inmates
- Inmate use of weapons
- Incidents in which cut or stab weapons were used

- Incidents in which minor, moderate, or major injuries were sustained by staff or inmates
- Incidents that officers resolved with the use of force
- Inmates involved in incidents who have no prior history of involvement in such activity
- Lawsuits filed
- Formal inmate complaints filed—any increase in the number of complaints should be evaluated in terms of patterns. Are there "hot" issues appearing time and again that need to be addressed immediately?
- Staff use of lethal force
- Attempted/successful escapes
- Walkaways from outside work details
- Failure to return from furlough
- Inmate demands to speak to the media
- Inmate found in possession of weapons
- Incidents of verbal defiance of staff
- Letters to the facility administrator and/or agency administrator (Freeman, 1996, p.60)

When taking into account the previous list of statistical indicators, it is evident that all correctional systems should have in place a standard reporting process (weekly or monthly) that directs every institution to furnish the main office with the statistics depicted here. Data analysis can render an early warning system by comparing each

Members of a SWAT Team performing a training exercise in Columbia, South Carolina.
(*Source:* South Carolina Department of Corrections – Mr. Al Waters' Collection)

report to former reports for each institution as well as comparing facilities to each other to ascertain if there are long-term statistical indicators of approaching problems (Freeman, 1996, p.60).

Inmates who are privileged about information that an inmate-precipitated exigency has been arranged may themselves partake in particular foretelling behaviors that are meaningful. These behaviors may intensify the affect produced by the identification of any of the long-term statistical indicators. Such behaviors may include the following:

Short-term Behavioral Observation Indicators
- Refusing to go to recreation, movies, or meals
- Warnings to family and friends not to visit the facility
- Hoarding of commissary items
- Increased levels of theft from the kitchen
- Mailing home of personal property items
- Cryptic warnings to staff to take a vacation or sick day
- Increased requests for antianxiety or antidepression medication
- Increased requests to be put in the infirmary or an outside hospital
- Increased requests for protective custody status in the disciplinary unit
- Unexpected changes in seating arrangements in the dining hall or race-, ethnic-, or gang-designated territory in the recreation yards
- Unusual levels of silence at recreation, movies, meals, or other regularly scheduled inmate activities
- Increased numbers of anonymous warnings that "something is about to happen"
- Increased numbers of transfer requests
- Avoidance of staff with whom a friendly relationship previously had been advanced
- Increased numbers of calls from family and friends about conditions in the facility
- Increased smuggling of contraband by visitors
- Increased number of requests for cell changes
- Polarization of known inmate rivals
- Grievance flooding—an extremely sharp increase in formal complaints all focused on one specific subject, usually an unpopular change in policy
- Increased suicide attempts (Freeman, 1996, p.60)

Changes in inmate conduct may be noticed by any category, level, or number of correctional employees. Alterations in behavior may be illustrated by a single inmate, a group of inmates, or for the entire inmate population. When an expansion in any of the behavioral observations or statistical data categories are analyzed, particularly if it is a distinct increase over a short period of time, the correctional institution's administrators at once should endeavor to recognize any essential patterns that may be contributing to these signs. Models of behavior to look for involve the following:

- A high frequency of involvement in violent incidents or complaints by a particular officer or inmate
- A commonly repeated complaint and/or any sign of coordination of complaint filing by specific inmates or groups
- Specific racial, ethnic, and gang involvement in a high percentage of incidents or complaints
- Specific locations in which a significant number of violent incidents are occurring
- Reaction to a planned or implemented policy change
- Significant changes in the inmate power structure (Freeman, 1996, p. 61)

Conclusion

The explanations for prison riots and disturbances are as numerous as the riots themselves. This chapter has examined eleven common groupings of reported causes of riots and disturbances that occurred in the United States between 1900 and 1995. The twelfth most frequently reported cause of prison riots is "multifactor" causation, which is examined in detail in Chapter 3.

Riot scene at Kirkland Correctional Institution, Columbia, South Carolina. (*Source:* South Carolina Department of Corrections – Mr. Al Waters' Collection)

As discussed in Chapter 1, these groupings are the underlying reported causes of prison riots that instigate a riot if there is a triggering event. Every prison is multifaceted. It is important to note that it is probably impossible to identify a single factor as the primary cause of a disruption in a prison environment. This environment is extremely diverse and complicated. There is always a level of hostility in an institution—it is not natural for human beings to be locked behind prison bars. Occasionally, a spark or a trigger will occur that will provide an opportunity for inmates to demonstrate how powerful and violent their hostility and frustration can be.

Prison Violence Caused by Multiple Events

Introduction

"Multiple-factor" causes set the stage leading to prison riots in 108 or 8 percent of the 1,334 prison riots that were reported to have occurred in the United States between 1900 and 1995. Reports indicate that almost half (42.86 percent) of all prison riots between 1900 and 1949 had multifactor causes. This number made up only twelve reported occurrences; however, there were only twenty-eight reported incidents during this period. There was a significant decrease in multifactor causes (15.76 percent or 61 of 387 reported incidents) between 1950 and 1979. This decrease continued into the period between 1980 and 1995 and dropped to 3.81 percent (35 of the reported 919 incidents). Experts offer different explanations for why this decrease occurred. Some suggested the primary reason was due to correctional staffs becoming more able to identify the "causes" of the violent incidents that they were experiencing.

> *"Brutalization begets brutalization, violence begets violence."*
>
> Dr. John Salazar
> former Secretary
> of Corrections
> State of New Mexico

Overview of Historical Views on Multifactor Causation

The following section presents an overview of various views on inmate life in prison. The authors contend that most of the elements involved in multiple-factor causation actually evolve from the treatment of inmates and their perceptions of their living conditions.

An early example of views concerning inmate life can be found in the first part of the 1800s. In 1881, Elam Lynds was appointed warden at Auburn prison and developed a new version of the "silent sys-

Riot scene at Kirkland Correctional Institution, Columbia, South Carolina.
(*Source:* South Carolina Department of Corrections – Mr. Al Waters' Collection)

tem," which previously had been used in the Pennsylvania Prison Model. His practice allowed inmates to interact during the day in congregate work areas, but to be separated into individual cells each night. In 1833, Lynds was interviewed about inmate discipline by Gestate de Beaumont and Alexis de Tocqueville, French writers who described early American society.

> I consider the chastisement by the whips the most efficient and at the same time the most humane which exists; it never injures health and obliges the prisoners to lead a life essentially healthy. . . . I consider it impossible to govern a large prison without a whip. Those who know human nature from books only may say the contrary (Clear and Cole, 1986, p. 76).

David E. Bright (1951), in his attempt to discover what influences, if any, have affected the personalities of prisoners during incarceration, found that, "The longer the time served in prison, the more adverse the attitudes of the inmates, and that better prison programs and facilities lead to better attitudes" (p. 84).

Another example can be found in the writings of Nathan Leopold. In his book, *Life Plus 99 Years* (1958), he reacted to the discomforts of the typical prison setting in the early to mid-1900s. He stated:

> The long period of being locked into one's cell from Saturday afternoon until Monday morning is one of the most disagreeable experiences in

prison. The physical surroundings, to begin with, are not particularly comfortable. The cells are very small: one can easily touch both side walls with outstretched arms. The bunk occupies well over half the available space; the stool and bucket account for almost half the remainder. The accumulated odors of nine hundred men confined in one building without plumbing facilities are definitely perceptible. Ventilation is poor; the light from the narrow windows in the outside wall, some thirty feet from the cells, is totally insufficient and the lights in the cells are always lit. There is a constant hum of talk and other incidental noise from the open cells (p. 161).

In 1972, Vernon Fox reported his views on the impact that prison conditions have on possible prison violence. He stated that:

Congressional debates and the majority of editorial opinion conclude that prison reform is necessary. Riots are evidence of stress and conflict within the institutions. The predisposing causes of riot, such as overcrowding and under-budgeting, must be handled both through legislative and administrative procedures, or it will be handled judicially. The precipitating causes can be generally corrected by up-grading the correctional officer so he can better handle minor incidents that could precipitate a riot. Better up-and-down communication between prison administration and staff on the one hand and prison inmates on the other can reduce the tension between them in the prison community (p. 41).

Additional views on prison conditions were found in historical congressional hearings that occurred in the United States in the early 1970s. The Select Committee on Crime reported in 1973 to the 93rd Congress that:

Prison riots are indications of long standing problems in our correctional institutions. Riots are significant because they tend to bring to public consciousness those aspects of prison life which are in most need of reform (U.S. House of Representatives, 1973, p. 3).

The Select Committee on Crime had investigated the Attica riot, in particular, and many other American prison riots. The Committee listed the following prison problem areas: inmate crowding, poor staff, rural prison location, lack of rehabilitative educational programs, meaningless employment, and insufficient vocational training.

The Committee also stated that:

> To force inmates to spend 16 to 24 hours a day in cells approximately 5 feet
> by 8 feet with no privacy, is the kind of dehumanizing practice which
> breeds hostility and unrest; it is this kind of treatment which sends embit-
> tered, un-rehabilitated prisoners back to a life of crime after release from
> prison. Overcrowding is common—almost the rule—in our nation's pris-
> ons and, based on the projections of the number of potential offenders who
> may become inmates, overcrowding in prisons is likely to be worse in the
> future (U.S. House of Representatives, 1973, p. 16).

In the 1970s, a class action suit was brought against the Metropolitan Correctional
Center (New York) by several of its inmates. The suit addressed the high level of
crowding of the institution. The minimum-security facility was intended to house
449 inmates (designed maximum capacity), each with an individual cell. However,
because of the level of incoming inmates and pretrial detainees, the practice of
double-bunking had been implemented throughout the facility.

Initially, the trial court found in favor of the inmates and stated that "compelling
necessity" was not displayed by institutional administrators in their treatment of the
overcrowding circumstances. However, on appeal, the Supreme Court reversed the
trial court's decision and instead held that "intent" should be the measurement by
which the court's decision is grounded. In other words, because prison officials had
not double-bunked inmates for punitive reasons, but, instead, had acted solely
out of a requirement to house inmates; therefore, the prisoner's Eighth Constitutional Amendment rights had not been violated. *Bell v. Wolfish*, 441 U.S. 520, 99 S.Ct.
1861 (1979).

The Select Committee on Crime further explored correctional problems and reported
that "prison staffs are undertrained, overworked, and not large enough to be effective" (U.S. House of Representatives, 1973, p. 17). The improper location of correctional facilities is another problem area that was identified:

> Prisons in rural localities suffer from an inability to secure adequate profes-
> sional staff from the surrounding countryside, and from a lack of access to
> work, study, and volunteer opportunities for prison rehabilitative pro-
> grams. Placing prisons in rural areas tends to isolate prisoners from their
> community ties and serves to further inmate dehumanization. This isola-
> tion tends to retard the rehabilitation of the prisoners (p. 17).

The lack of rehabilitative educational programs is a problem situation for prisons. An Attica inmate testified before this Committee that:

> It took my own compulsion for me to rehabilitate myself. I had to pay money to get a correspondence course because the state refused to let me continue my education, because they said, "Well, you're a high school graduate, so there's no need for you to pursue any college courses." . . . You can hardly get a job out here if you haven't finished high school. So, now, all the time you spent in prison, you spent it vegetating. Why? Because everybody says rehabilitation looks good on paper, but nobody's supplying it (p. 24).

The Select Committee on Crime stressed the need for meaningful employment and adequate vocational training. The Committee stated that:

> Establishing meaningful work programs for inmates provides an opportunity for inmates to contribute to their own, and perhaps their dependents' support. On the other hand, idleness in correctional institutions involves a needless waste of the taxpayers' money because inmates supported at public expense are neither engaged in productive work nor given an opportunity to learn a trade or occupation to help them become self-supporting upon release. It undermines inmate and staff morale, creates unrest and disciplinary problems, and generates apathy, contempt and cynicism toward any genuine rehabilitative efforts (p. 29).

When looking at multifactor causation, researchers have found that people today, in general (especially inmates), are more likely to question authority; at the same time, those who are incarcerated also have to deal with their confinement and the reduction of personal liberty that prison life brings. There have been several occurrences (American Correctional Association, 1990a) since World War II that have shown this: the Vietnam War (which caused many to question the actions of the American government); the Civil Rights Movement (which raised concerns of racial conflict and societal protest); the assassination of Dr. Martin Luther King, Jr.; and the general decline of many cities that have become areas of high unemployment and unrest in the 1980s and 1990s.

Examples of Prison Violence Caused by Multiple Events

Prisons riots often are caused by multiple events. For example, Sing Sing Prison in New York had a riot on July 23, 1913. The two reported causes were inmate inactivity (following a lockup after a fire) and poor food. This riot lasted seventy hours and resulted in $150,000 worth of damages due to fires and smashed windows. During the climax of the riot, one inmate was killed by another inmate. The occurrence ended when the warden listened to grievances and promised amnesty for those who cooperated with him. Also, the "tougher" prisoners were transferred to Auburn Prison in New York.

The Philadelphia County Prison in Pennsylvania was the scene of a riot on January 13, 1929. The riot involved 600 inmates. The reported causes were poor food, mistreatment, and bad living conditions. The riot lasted for two and one-half hours and resulted in $10,000 worth of damages. Tear gas was used to end the riot.

Southern Michigan Prison had a riot on April 21, 1952. One hundred and sixty-nine inmates were involved. The reported causes were beating of mentally ill inmates by inmate nurses, stopping the delivery of personal mail, placing criminal sexual psychopaths among the general population, and placing inmates with epilepsy and tuberculosis in cells instead of hospitals. The riot cost $3,000,000 in damages. It lasted for five days with one inmate being killed and fifteen inmates injured. The riot ended when the Governor accepted an eleven-point reform demand and promised no reprisals against prisoners by correctional officers or other personnel.

The Oregon State Penitentiary had a riot on July 12, 1953. Eight hundred inmates were involved in this riot which lasted three days. The reported causes were a reprisal against guards who had broken up the previous day's raid on the food supply, inmate demands for more and better food, demands for better dining room sanitation, an end to the policy of holding back a portion of pay until release, and a request for the discharge of a hospital attendant. The riot caused damage of $100,000 and one inmate was injured.

Walla Walla State Prison in the State of Washington was the scene of a riot on July 6, 1955. The riot lasted 26 hours and involved 800 inmates. The reported causes were inmate demands for investigation of the parole board, a request that men in segregation be moved and their slates wiped clean, the creation of an inmate council, prompt acknowledgment of the request to see officials, the removal of the head of classification, and the securing of an attorney to give legal assistance to inmates. The riot ended when a nine-point agreement was signed with inmates.

A riot occurred at Central Prison in North Carolina on April 18, 1968. Four hundred inmates participated in the riot. The reported causes of the riot were anger of powerful inmates about a drive to rid the prison of racketeering, inmates desire for extended time to watch television, inmates desire for three hot meals a day, demands for longer visiting hours, and crowded conditions. Five inmates were killed during the riot. Injuries were sustained by seventy-eight inmates, two state police, and three correctional officers.

The final report of the South Carolina Department of Corrections' *Collective Violence Research Project* (1973) describes a riot which occurred at the Central Correctional Institution, in Columbia, South Carolina, on October 2, 1968. This riot involved 300 inmates. Grievances about more and better food, dismissal of four officials, the need for central air conditioning, and access to reporters were the reported causes of the riot. Damages of the riot were said to be $57,950. Injuries were sustained by eleven inmates and six correctional officers (South Carolina Department of Corrections, 1973).

The Raiford State Prison in Raiford, Florida was the setting for a prison riot on February 13, 1971. This riot involved 600 inmates, including 64 who were injured. The reported causes included inmate demands: for conjugal visits, better food, lockers and tables in cells, better vocational training, improved parole procedures, the right to keep hobby supplies in cells, payment for prison work, and more programs by outside entertainment.

On April 28, 1971, a riot erupted at the Essex County Jail in New Jersey. Two hundred inmates participated in it. Two inmates and four correctional officers were injured. The reported causes included inmate grievances about crowding, high bail, lack of recreational facilities, and dietary practices.

One of the most famous prison riots involving multiple causes occurred at the Attica Correctional Facility in Attica, New York. This riot lasted from September 9 to September 13, 1971. A total of 1,281 inmates were involved in this riot which resulted in 32 inmates and 11 staff being killed (New York State Special Commission on Attica, 1972). On September 8, an inmate attacked a correctional officer. The inmate felt he had been harassed. The following day after eating breakfast, inmates refused to return to their cells. Inmates obtained weapons and began taking over cellblocks. Correctional officers and staff were attacked, and fifty individuals were taken hostage (eleven were released after one hour). Property was destroyed. Officials later estimated the damages in excess of $3 million.

Inmate leaders agreed to meet with Commissioner Russell Oswald and a committee of thirty-seven observers. The inmates had a list of twenty-eight demands. Some of the demands included complete amnesty from prosecution; provision of adequate food, shelter, and clothing; allowance of true religious freedom with no censorship; institution of rehabilitation, education, drug, legal, and employment programs; reduction of cell time; provision of better medical treatment; reduced discipline for inmates in segregation and for parole violators; and assurance that Attica would be reconstructed by inmates.

The spokesman for the inmates was a tall, twenty-one-year-old black man from Rochester, New York, Elliot James Barkley. He once had been imprisoned for drug use and had a previous record of cashing forged money orders (when he was eighteen years old he cashed an order for $124.60 and had been sent to Elmira Reformatory for four years). In January 1970, Barkley was paroled at which time he returned to Rochester where he again was arrested for driving without a license, a violation of his parole that caused his parole to be revoked, and he was sent to the maximum-security prison, Attica. In this institution, Barkley became perhaps the most well-known inmate orator in history. After the breakout of the Attica riot in D-yard, Barkley was joined by Richard Clark, another inmate leader, in being elected to represent the A-block inmates within the institution.

> Nonviolent inmate disturbances include hunger strikes, sit-down strikes, work stoppages, voluntary lockdowns . . . excessive numbers of inmates reporting for sick call, and the filing of grievances by nearly everyone in a cellblock or even in the entire institution. Violent inmate disturbances include . . . assaulting officers; sabotaging the electrical, plumbing, or heating systems; burning or destroying institutional property; and taking control, with or without hostages, of a cellblock, a yard, or an entire prison (Clemens Bartollas and John Conrad, 1992).

The official causes of the Attica riot were brutality of correctional officers to black and Hispanic inmates, increased political militancy among black inmates, the death of inmate leader George Jackson at San Quentin, prison conditions as pointed out in their twenty-eight demands, crowding (the facility was designed for 1,200 inmates, but 2,243 inmates were there at the time of the riot), and idleness. New York State Troopers retook Attica after four days of failed negotiations. The majority of deaths occurred in the retaking of the prison.

On November 25, 1971, a prison riot took place at the Rahway State Prison in New Jersey. Officials report that between 500 and 600 inmates were involved in this riot in which six hostages were held. The reported causes of this riot were extensive: a demand for new hearings before the parole board, an end of the seven-day work week, better medical care, proper diet, lower commissary prices, religious freedom, work-release programs, rehabilitation programs, an end to discrimination, better food, faster mail service, higher wages, and expense money for inmates.

The Fox Lake Correctional Institution in Fox Lake, Wisconsin, experienced a riot on June 13, 1977. The following causes were listed: unrest marked by talk of employee strikes, undifferentiated inmate complaints, and aggressive inmate leaders. The riot involved sixty inmates and lasted two hours. Property damage amounted to $100,000. Thirty-two hostages were taken; eventually, the riot was ended by use of force. Only minor injuries were reported.

On February 2, 1980, a riot broke out at the Penitentiary of New Mexico in Santa Fe. The inmate population at this institution was 1,157 at the time of the riot. The prison was designed for 974 inmates. The Attorney General's report listed the following items as causes of the riot: crowding, understaffed security, correctional officer harassment, poor food, overall poor conditions of the institution, a poor classification process, and a lack of incentives for inmates.

The riot started on February 2, when inmates in dorm E-2 attacked four correctional officers during a routine inspection. Many inmates had been drinking homebrew prior to the riot. Inmates took keys from the correctional officers and released inmates in other dorms. The "unbreakable" glass surrounding the control center was broken by the rioting inmates. Inmates also gained access to the maximum-security unit, the medical unit, the protective custody unit (where many "snitches" were tortured to death), the tool room (where welding torches were seized and used on inmates who were "snitches"), and the records room.

The majority of the inmates escaped to outside areas and did not participate. Inmates set fires and destroyed buildings. The legislature of New Mexico appropriated $87,500,000 to build new institutions after this riot. The riot lasted thirty-six hours. The National Guard, SWAT, and local police regained control of the institution without incident. Thirty-three inmates were killed in this riot by other inmates. Inmate informants (snitches) were a major target of the rioting inmates. An estimated total of 150 inmates took part in the riot. Twelve hostages were taken.

Inmate demands included: allowing inmates the opportunity to speak to the news media; bringing in federal officials to insure no retaliation; reconstructing the classification process; easing crowding; improving visiting conditions, prison food, and recreational and educational facilities; appointing a new disciplinary committee; and ending overall harassment.

On March 15, 1982, a prison riot occurred at the Perry Correctional Institution in Pelzer, South Carolina. Approximately seventy-five inmates took part in this riot, which lasted four hours. No hostages were taken. The listed reported causes were lack of health care, high canteen prices, poor food service, strict visitation privileges, and poor mail delivery. There was damage to the canteen and stolen items from the commissary in the amount of $2,200; three television monitors were destroyed; a vehicle was damaged; and drums of soap were poured out.

The riot ended when the inmates were instructed to return to their dorms, list their complaints, and select two representatives from each maximum-security dorm to air their complaints. On the same day, the warden, deputy warden, and two chief correctional officers met with the inmate representatives (approximately ten) to discuss their complaints.

On September 10, 1983, a disturbance took place at the Joe Harp Correctional Center in Lexington, Oklahoma. The two reported causes were racial tension and disproportional food service. Prison officials reported that Indian food servers handed lesser portions to black inmates. This created an argument that continued onto the prison baseball field afterwards. Fights broke out between inmates and caused a forty-five minute disturbance. Forty-four inmates were involved and property damage (mostly broken windows) was $35,000.

The U.S. Penitentiary in Atlanta, Georgia, experienced a prison riot on November 23, 1987. Cuban detainees in Atlanta had been upset for a long time about their living conditions. This riot happened two days after the riot in the Oakdale Detention Center in Oakdale, California. The Cuban detainees at Oakdale rioted when they learned of United States plans to reactivate the emigration accord and send them back to Cuba. Inmates in Oakdale took twenty-eight hostages and burned more than half of the forty-seven-acre complex.

A congressional subcommittee chaired by Representative Robert Kastenmeier had reported:

> The current living situation for the Cubans at the Atlanta Federal Penitentiary is intolerable considering even the most minimal correctional standards. These detainees—who are virtually without legal rights—are worse off than virtually all other federal sentenced inmates. They are required to live in conditions which are brutal and inhumane. They are confined without any practical hope of ever being released. These conditions . . . present a strong possibility of future violent confrontations. For these reasons alone, Congress and the administration should be motivated to seek out a constructive solution (Hamm, 1995, p.89).

On February 1, 1988, the subcommittee also concluded in a report to the Attorney General on disturbances at the Federal Detention Center, Oakdale, Louisiana, and the U.S. Penitentiary, Atlanta, Georgia, that:

> (1) Of the 1,869 Mariel (Cuban) detainees incarcerated at the prison, none was serving criminal sentences. That is, the detainees had already

served their sentences for criminal transgressions, or they had committed no crimes at all.

(2) The prison was estimated to be 45 percent overcrowded—the worst crowding conditions among the fifty-nine institutions in the federal prison system. Detainees in Cell Houses A and B were being housed eight to a cell, with an average space of seven feet by four feet per inmate. Each cell included a toilet without a partition, a sink, and four bunk beds. Detainees in Cell Houses B, C, and E were confined to their cells twenty-three hours a day. Warden Hanberry acknowledged to Kastenmeier that these conditions were far below those set out in the American Correctional Association's current *Manual of Standards*.

(3) Violence was considered a "significant problem." From January 1982 through February 1986, there had been seven suicides among the detainees; the total would rise to nine by November 1987. There had also been 158 serious suicide attempts, more than two thousand serious incidents of self-mutilation, nine homicides, and at least ten deaths from heart attacks and other "natural causes." The inmate-on-inmate assault rate among the detainees averaged fifteen per month, more than half the total for the entire Bureau of Prisons population. The number of inmate-on-staff assaults ranged from eleven to forty-one per month, accounting for about one-third of the Bureau's total. In 1984 and 1985, the number of inmate-on-staff assaults referred by Atlanta officials to the U.S. District Attorney had increased from five to fifty.

(4) Approximately two hundred detainees (about 11 percent of the total population) were classified as mentally retarded, mentally disordered, or psychotic. Another 587 detainees (31 percent of the total) had medical problems of some kind. Most of these infirm detainees were locked in Cell House C, where they were administered daily doses of psychotropic medication (either Lithium or Haldol).

(5) Of the 518 employees of the Atlanta prison, only about a hundred (fewer than 20 percent) spoke Spanish.

(6) The average staff turnover rate was one of the highest in the federal prison system. Atlanta staff also had the highest rate of sick leave and the highest disciplinary rate of any staff in the system. Hanberry attributed these problems to the severe conditions of employment and the increased level of stress brought on by the 1984 disturbance.

(7) Since the 1984 disturbance, all staff had been put on mandatory twelve-hour shifts

(8) The cost of housing Mariel (Cuban) detainees at the prison was estimated at $40 million per year—roughly $240 million during the period 1981 to 1986 (Hamm, 1995).

The Cuban detainees in Atlanta on November 23, 1987 took 102 hostages. Three buildings were burned. Damages at Oakdale and Atlanta were estimated at $113.5 million dollars.

On November 29, 1987, Auxiliary Bishop Augustin Roman of Miami met with Cuban detainees at Oakdale, California. Within an hour, he convinced them to lay down their weapons and surrender all hostages. On December 2, 1987, Bishop Roman delivered a three-minute audiotape to the Atlanta detainees. The next day, December 3, the Atlanta detainees voted to end the ten-day siege. On December 4, 1987, Bishop Roman facilitated the signing of an agreement to end the crisis.

A Pennsylvania prison riot took place at the Camp Hill Correctional Institution on October 25, 1989. The major causes of the riot were prison crowding, poor staff training, inmate concern about medical care, and inmate anger due to a change in visitation rules. The institution was designed for 1,800 inmates but housed 2,600 inmates at the time of the riot.

Inmates started fires which resulted in $3 million dollars worth of damages. Seventeen staff members were taken hostage. On October 27, 1989, the riot was terminated by state police entering the institution. A day earlier, inmates had given up after negotiating with prison officials. A second riot started soon afterwards in the institution because inmates had been confined to unsecured cells. This riot was ended by force.

On September 22, 1991, the maximum-security unit at the Montana State Prison had a disturbance. Nine inmates were involved. Inmates involved were mainly long-term inmates who had been in the maximum unit for four years or more. They complained about lack of programs and activities and being locked in their cells twenty-three hours a day. Other concerns of these inmates included the limited access to the phones, poor food, abuse from staff, and the grievance system. No staff were injured. However, five staff were taken hostage. Five inmates were killed in this disturbance. They had been housed in the protective custody block of the unit. Property damage amounted to approximately $100,000. Inmate property and staff property in the maximum-security unit were damaged.

The disturbance was ended by the Disturbance Control Team. The team pried open the roof escape hatches and threw small pyrotechnic tear gas canisters into the maximum-security unit. Inmates were ordered to strip and lie down in place on the floor. The team secured one block at a time in regaining control of the building.

SWAT Team performing a training exercise in Columbia, South Carolina.
(*Source:* South Carolina Department of Corrections – Mr. William Crawley's Collection)

On April 11, 1993, at 3 PM, a riot took place in Lucasville, Ohio, at the Southern Ohio Correctional Facility. This riot, which lasted eleven days, is also known as the Easter Riot. A major complaint of the rioting inmates was the requirement by prison officials that inmates take part in the tuberculin skin test program. Many inmates felt this process conflicted with their religious beliefs. Other concerns of the inmates prior to the riot were crowding, lack of inmate programs, and increased use of tighter security procedures in the institution.

Four inmate gang leaders influenced the progression of the riot, which resulted in the deaths of nine inmates and one correctional officer. L-Block was destroyed, and it cost approximately $26 million to rebuild the institution. The riot was resolved by negotiation.

On May 4, 1993, a riot occurred at the Cameron-Morrison Youth Institution in Hoffman, North Carolina. This two-day riot involved fifty inmates and resulted in property damages estimated at $1,000. There were several predisposing conditions: lack of single cell segregation space, custody staff were tired due to considerable overtime due to staff shortages, reduction in structured recreation programs, passive staff response to long-term inmates, the race ratio at the facility was imbalanced, home town cliques developed, and minor incidents were not handled effectively. The riot ended by a show of force and an ultimatum from the Emergency Response Team.

Conclusion

The American Correctional Association (1990a) traditionally has felt that some of the following problem areas can increase the chances of a multifactored riot occurring: failure to control contraband, frequent turnover of staff, poor communication, frequent changes in policies, lack of meaningful programs, improper classification, poor responses to inmate complaints, unclear rules, failure to respond to high levels of inmate-to-inmate and inmate-to-staff incidents, vague lines of authority, crowding, and high-level administrators who are not available to inmates and staff.

Many research studies and federal investigations (DiIulio, 1989; Marquart, 1989; and U.S. Department of Justice, 1991) have found that the "quality of prison management" had the largest impact on establishing the "quality of prison life." In the research conducted for this book, we determined that the "quality of prison life" probably will have the greatest impact on whether a prison riot will occur. We suggest that the "quality of prison life" is probably the main component in multifactored prison riots.

We hope that prison management and security will advance to the point that Attica-type riots will be seen only in history books. The following description of Attica is a painful reminder of the deadly costs of prison riots.

> Forty-three citizens of New York State died at Attica Correctional Facility between September 9 and 13, 1971. Thirty-nine of that number were killed and more than 80 others were wounded by gunfire during the 15 minutes it took the State Police to retake the prison on September 13. With the exception of Indian massacres in the late 19th century, the State Police assault which ended the four-day prison uprising was the bloodiest one-day encounter between Americans since the Civil War (New York State Special Commission on Attica, 1972).

Analysis of Prison Violence from 1900 to 1995

Introduction: Historical Trends

This chapter presents the results of national research on the characteristics and triggering events of all reported prison riots from 1900 to 1995. Many interesting trends emerged from this historical research. These trends will be examined along with the twelve common groupings for prison riot-triggering events discussed in other chapters.

Readers should keep in mind several issues surrounding the "reporting" described in this chapter:

- The reported precipitating condition of a riot was in actuality a "trigger" for the violence that followed.

- How a situation was reported probably was very dependent on the person who did the reporting.

- How a situation was reported probably was very dependent on where (geographically) the situation occurred.

- How a situation was reported probably was very dependent on the decade when the situation occurred.

With this in mind, the following is an examination of the 1,334 prison riots reported in the United States from 1900 to 1995.

> *"There's always time to die. I don't know what the rush was."*
>
> Congressman Herman Badillo
> Member of the negotiation team at
> Attica Riot in 1971

Number of Incidents by Reported Cause

Figure 4.1 depicts the reported causes of prison riots based on frequency from the years 1900 to 1995. The total number of reported incidents between 1900 and 1995 was 1,334.

Figure 4.1. American Prison Riots 1900 to 1995
Number of Incidents by Reported Causes

	Number	Percentage
Conflict with other inmate	399	29.91
Unknown cause	227	17.02
Rules/regulations violations	208	15.60
Racial tension	141	10.57
Multiple factors	108	8.10
Gang related	56	4.20
Security issues	46	3.45
Confrontation with staff	45	3.45
Institutional food	42	3.15
Mass escape attempts	25	1.88
Alcohol and drug-related	19	1.42
Rumors	18	1.35
Total	1,334	100%*

*The total may not equal 100 percent due to rounding.

Note that in Figure 4.1, the top five reported causes of a violent prison occurrence comprised 81.20 percent of the "explanations" for the 1,334 reported riots experienced in the United States from 1900 and 1995. It is not surprising that "confrontation with other inmates" (29.91 percent) led the list in reported prison violence. Nor is it surprising that "unknown" (17.02 percent) would be the second-most reported cause. Of course, it could be argued that these incidents probably were influenced by one of the other "events" listed, but due to the particular situation encountered, there were 227 occurrences for which no clear cause could be identified or was reported.

> Riots can happen anywhere and to anyone. A riot must be stopped before it can expand to become uncontrollable.
>
> *Ken McKeller*
> *Division Director of Security*
> *South Carolina Department of Corrections*

Many of the areas often perceived as the main factors that influenced prison violence were at the bottom of the reported list instead of the top. "Institutional food" is a frequently expected cause of prison violence in the United States. In this particular study, food was identified as the cause of forty-two incidents or 3.15 percent of all reported occurrences between 1900 and 1995. Mass-escape attempts are often a concern of the general public when a violent event occurs. However, this research discovered that escape attempts were the reported cause of twenty-five prison riots, 1.88 percent of all reported occurrences, during the ninety-five year period studied.

One area that made the top twelve reported cause of prison riots was "rumors." Interestingly, eighteen incidents in the United States during this time period were reported as being caused solely by rumors passed from inmate to inmate. Such rumors most often dealt with "information" about the mistreatment and even murder of other inmates in their particular institution.

Types of Reported Underlying Causes of Prison Riots

1900 to 1949

Figure 4.2 shows the types of reported causes of prison riots from 1900 to 1949. Twenty-eight of the 1,334 reported prison-violence incidents occurred between 1900 and 1949.

Figure 4.2. Types of Reported "Underlying Causes" of Prison Riots from 1900 to 1949

	Number	Percentage
Multiple factors	12	42.86
Rules/regulation violations	9	32.14
Unknown causes	4	14.29
Racial tension	1	3.57
Institutional food	1	3.57
Mass escape attempt	1	3.57
Totals	28	100%

Between 1900 and 1949, the most commonly reported underlying cause of a prison riot was that of "multiple factors." A close second with respect to the most reported event during this fifty-year period was inmate conflict with institutional rules and regulations. These conflicts either came from inmate dissatisfaction with the rules or from physical confrontations with staff who were attempting to force inmate compliance with rules or regulations. Racial tension, problems with institutional food, and a mass escape attempt were the least-frequently reported underlying causes with only one reported incident each.

1950 to 1979

Figure 4.3. Types of Reported Underlying Causes of Prison Riots from 1950 to 1979

	Number	Percentage
Rules or regulations violations	102	26.36
Unknown causes	83	21.45
Multiple factors	61	15.76
Racial tension	59	15.24
Security issues	16	4.13
Mass escape attempts	14	3.62
Institutional food	13	3.36
Confrontation with other inmates	10	2.58
Alcohol and drug related	9	2.33
Rumors	9	2.33
Confrontation with staff	7	1.80
Gang related	4	1.03
Totals	387	100%*

*The total may not equal 100 percent due to rounding.

Figure 4.3 shows the types of causes of violent prison incidents from 1950 to 1979. Of the reported prison violence incidents, 387 occurred between 1950 and 1979. During this time period, inmate conflict with rules and regulations was the number one reported cause of prison riots.

At the end of 1996, the total number of inmates imprisoned in both federal and state adult correctional institutions was 1,182,169. Overall, America's prison population grew by 5 percent, which was less than the average annual growth rate of 7.3 percent recorded since 1990. The 1996 increase was the equivalent of 1,075 more inmates per week. Relative to the number of United States' residents, the rate of incarceration in prisons during this time period totaled 427 sentenced inmates per 100,000 residents, up from 292 in 1990 (Bureau of Justice Statistics, June 1997).

Starting in the 1950s, "racial tension" began to increase, and eventually was reported to be a major mechanism of prison riots. Racial tension as a reported cause was at its highest in the 1970s. It is not clear why racial tension was not reported until this time period. It is doubtful that it only began to be an issue in these decades. Perhaps this is reflective of the problems discussed in the "Overview of Problems Surrounding Riots Research," in Chapter One of this book (including accuracy of reporting, lack of an inclusive system, societal values, temporal displacement, advances in communications, computer technology, transportation, and spatial displacement).

1980 to 1995

Figure 4.4 displays the types and numbers of reported causes of prison riots from 1980 to 1995, when 919 incidents occurred.

Figure 4.4. Types of Reported Causes of Prison Violence from 1980 to 1995

	Number	Percentage
Confrontation with other inmates	389	42.33
Unknown causes	140	15.23
Rules or regulations violations	97	10.56
Racial tension	81	8.81
Gang related	52	5.66
Confrontation with staff	38	4.13
Multiple factors	35	3.81
Security issues	30	3.26
Institutional food	28	3.05
Mass escape attempts	10	1.09
Alcohol and drug related	10	1.09
Rumors	9	0.98
Totals	919	100%*

*The total may not equal 100 percent due to rounding.

During the fifteen years from 1980 to 1995, there was more prison violence (919 incidents) than all of the other decades combined (415). The 389 incidents of conflict with other inmates was the number one reported cause for prison violence during this period. We may assume that many of these conflicts probably were race related, but racial tension as the primary factor of a particular incident was reported in only 81 of these 919 reported incidents. Of the 140 reported incidents, occurrences with no particular primary cause continued to be in the top three category. During this time period, the fifty-two incidents involving gangs indicated that gangs had become a growing reported cause for prison riots. "Gangs" as a separate factor in prison violence had emerged in the late 1970s.

Interestingly, riots caused by conflict with correctional staff declined in the 1980s, and the trend appears to be continuing into the 1990s. This could be a positive sign of the times and possibly a result of the increased attention given to correctional officer training, staff and inmate communication, and grievance systems.

Summary of Trends from 1900 to 1995

During this ninety-five year period, five trends became evident. Three trends increased: "Confrontation with Other Inmates", "Confrontation with Staff" and "Gang Related" issues. These were reported as the incidents that served as the final "trigger" for the occurrence of the violent event. The seven other reported events (unknown causes, racial tension, institutional food, and so forth) showed no clear trends; they increased and decreased randomly during this ninety-five year period.

"Confrontation with Other Inmates"

The trend that increased by the greatest percentage was "Confrontation with Other Inmates." From 1900 to 1949, no prison riot reports said conflicts between inmates was the sole cause of a riot or disturbance. However, the twelve riots, or 42.86 percent of the total number of incidents occurring during this time period, labeled "Multiple factor," could have been caused by conflicts between inmates, but the incident was not reported as the cause. In addition, there was also one incident that was reported to have been ignited from "racial tension," which, of course, is an additional indication that conflict between inmates did exist.

Not until the period 1950-1979 was the conflict between inmates reported as a cause of a riot (a 2.58 percent increase). Then, ten violent incidents were reported as a result of this type of conflict. Between this time period and the 1980 and early 1990s, there would be a 39.75 percent increase in the number of incidents reported as attributable to conflict between inmates. From 1980 to 1995, there were 389 reported instances (42.33 percent of the 919 incidents that occurred in this period) of prison violence that evolved from conflict between inmates.

"Confrontation with Staff"

Conflict between inmates and staff was another reported cause that did not come to light until the time period of 1950 to 1979. During this time period, this issue was reported as the primary cause in only 7 (1.80 percent) of the 387 reported incidents. There was a slight increase in this category (4.13 percent) during the 1980 to 1995 year period.

"Gang Related"

Conflict between gangs, or individual members of a prison gang, as a reported cause was the third and final area that increased during this time period. There were no reports of gangs in prison as a primary problem until the 1970s (when they comprised 1.03 percent of the violent incidents between 1950 and 1979). This would increase to 5.66 percent of the reported causes reported between 1980 and 1995 (52 of the 919 reported violent prison incidents).

"Rules, Regulations, Policies, Crowding, and Actions of Prison Officials"

Two events exhibit very distinct decreases in their percentages of being reported. Between 1900 and 1949, "Rules and regulations violations" was reported as the primary cause in 32.14 percent (9) of the violent incidents that occurred. This number increased to 102 reports between 1950 and 1979, but this was only 26.36 percent of the overall percentage of riots during this period. This percentage continued to decrease between 1980 and 1995, dropping to only 10.56 percent (97 of the 919 occurrences) of the reported violent incidents and riots.

"Multiple Factors"

A multiple-factor cause was an underlying cause leading to prison riots in almost half (42.86 percent) of all the prison violence incidents between 1900 and 1949. This number made up only 12 reported occurrences; however, there were only 28 reported incidents during this period. This percentage significantly decreased (15.76 percent or 61 of 387 reported incidents) between 1950 and 1979. This decrease continued into the period between 1980 and 1995 and dropped to 3.81 percent (35 of the reported 919 incidents). Authorities offer different explanations for why this decrease occurred. Many contend that the most likely reason was due to correctional staffs becoming more able to identify the causes of the violent incidents that they were experiencing.

Temporal and Spatial Trends in Causes of Prison Violence

Reported American Prison Violence Incidents by Decade of Occurrence

Figure 4.5 displays the number of prison riots from 1900 to 1995. To make the data more understandable, we organized it into ten-year periods, with the exception of the first and last entry.

Figure 4.5. Number of Reported American Prison Riots per Decade

	Decade Number	Percentage
1900 to 1919	10	0.75
1920 to 1929	13	0.97
1930 to 1939	1	0.07
1940 to 1949	4	0.30
1950 to 1959	87	6.52
1960 to 1969	58	4.35
1970 to 1979	242	18.14
1980 to 1989	524	39.28
1990 to 1995	395	29.61
Totals	1,334	100%

Several trends become evident in an analysis of this data. In each decade, there was an acceleration in the number of reported prison incidents and riots, with the exception of 1930 to 1949, but the increases displayed some inconsistency. For example, steady increases occurred; then, a sudden decrease in the number of reported incidents followed in the next ten-year period. Possibly, this could have been due to a lack of reporting or other technical problems. On the other hand, the inmates might have been concerned with other societal issues instead of "rioting" (in other words, the Depression of the 1930s or World War II during the 1940s). The largest increase in reported prison violence occurred between the late 1960s and early to mid-1970s. With the unrest in the country at this time, it was not surprising to see this massive increase from 58 riots to 242.

Since 1970, the number of reported prison riots and incidents has doubled with each new decade. There were 242 reported events in the 1970s and almost double that number (524) in the 1980s. The first five years of the 1990s shows that this trend likely will continue.

Reported American Prison Violence Incidents by Month of Occurrence

The following chart displays the number of reported prison riots and incidents that occurred in the various months of the years from 1900 to 1995.

Figure 4.6. Reported American Prison Riots and Incidents by Month of Occurrence 1900 to 1995*

Month	Number
January	85
February	58
March	75
April	90
May	101
June	82
July	124
August	125
September	99
October	96
November	171
December	176
Total Reported Incidents	1,282

* 52 riots were reported without the month of their occurrence

Figure 4.6 presents research findings that are contrary to the common perception with respect to the time of year when most riots occur. Usually, people assume that the summer months, due to the heat and humid weather, produce the largest number of riots across the country in any given year. However, research revealed that the summer months (July and August) displayed only the second-highest frequency of reported prison riots. The months of December (176) and November (171) had the largest number of reported occurrences from 1900 to 1995. There may be many different explanations for these findings. Perhaps, the feelings around the holiday seasons may have had more of an impact on inmates than the heat of the summer months. Adding to this frustration may have been less outdoor activity (time in the yard) for the inmates.

Reported American Prison Violence Incidents by State of Occurrence

Figure 4.7. Frequency of Prison Riots Experienced by Individual States
(Total of 1,334 Reported Riots from 1900 to 1995)

State	Number	State	Number
Alabama	6	Montana	7
Alaska	0	Nebraska	18
Arizona	17	Nevada	8
Arkansas	4	New Hampshire	2
California	460	New Jersey	38
Colorado	18	New Mexico	13
Connecticut	25	New York	47
Delaware	9	North Carolina	30
District of Columbia	3	North Dakota	0
Florida	48	Ohio	20
Georgia	46	Oklahoma	22
Hawaii	7	Oregon	10
Idaho	10	Pennsylvania	45
Illinois	17	Rhode Island	7
Indiana	40	South Carolina	19
Iowa	10	South Dakota	8
Kansas	21	Tennessee	16
Kentucky	19	Texas	63
Louisiana	14	Utah	9
Maine	2	Vermont	0
Maryland	23	Virginia	38
Massachusetts	12	Washington	30
Michigan	11	West Virginia	5
Minnesota	14	Wisconsin	9
Mississippi	13	Wyoming	2
Missouri	19		

Figure 4.7 lists the number of reported prison riots in each state between 1900 and 1995. The six states with the largest number of reported violent occurrences are the following:

California	460
Texas	63
Florida	48
New York	47
Georgia	46
Pennsylvania	45

Wide variance existed in the number of reported incidents experienced by individual states during this time period. Alaska, North Dakota, and Vermont, reported no violent incidents occurring during this ninety-five year period. Not surprisingly, California reported the highest number of occurrences, 460. The State of Texas was a distant second with sixty-three reported incidents. Eighteen states and the District of Columbia experienced between one and ten violent occurrences during this period of time. Six states experienced between twenty-one and thirty riots. Thirteen states experienced between eleven and twenty riots.

SWAT Team performing a training exercise in Columbia, South Carolina.
(*Source:* South Carolina Department of Corrections – Mr. William Crawley's Collection)

Trends of Interaction and Termination

Length of Occurrences

Violent prison incidents between 1900 and 1995 varied in duration from 20 minutes to over 260 hours. Figure 4.8 shows this variance in duration.

Figure 4.8. Distribution of American Prison Riots and Disturbances by Duration from 1900 to 1995*

	Number	Percentage
Less than 1 hour	40	11.43
1 hour to 2 hours, 59 minutes	78	22.29
3 hours to 5 hours, 59 minutes	70	20.00
6 hours to 8 hours, 59 minutes	41	11.71
9 hours to 11 hours, 59 minutes	13	3.71
12 hours to 14 hours, 59 minutes	8	2.29
15 hours to 17 hours, 59 minutes	9	2.57
18 hours to 20 hours, 59 minutes	4	1.14
21 hours to 23 hours, 59 minutes	6	1.71
24 hours to 35 hours, 59 minutes	26	7.43
36 hours to 47 hours, 59 minutes	8	2.29
48 hours and above	47	13.43
Totals	350	100%**

*Duration not reported in 984 incidents
**Total may not equal 100 percent due to rounding.

Of the 1,334 reported prison riots, information about the duration of a particular occurrence was reported in only 350 instances. With this data, it would appear that almost half (42.29 percent) of the sample had a duration of between one and five hours. Forty-seven (13.43 percent) of the reported riots lasted forty-eight hours or more.

Riot-termination Methods

How a prison riot was resolved or terminated was reported in only 255 of the 1,334 incidents. How the incident ended was not reported in 1,079 of the reported occurrences from 1900 to 1995. Of the 255 occurrences on which data was available, negotiation occurred in 55 cases and did not occur in the other 200. As shown in Figure 4.9, whether negotiation with inmates occurred or not, "use of force" and "show of force" were reported as the first and second most-used termination method, respectively. "Use of force" was reported in seventy-two (28.23 percent) occurrences and "show of force" was reported sixty-three times (24.70 percent) as the chosen method for riot termination. "Negotiation with inmates" was a close third, being used in fifty-five incidents (21.56 percent). "Use of chemical agents" was fourth and cited as a separate termination method in twenty-nine (11.37 percent) of the reported occurrences. Interestingly, in almost 10 percent of the reported riots, inmates voluntarily surrendered without any intervention by outside sources. "Threats by prison administration" was the sixth response, and was reported in 12 (4.70 percent) of the reported incidents.

Figure 4.9. Distribution of American Prison Riots and Disturbances 1990-1995 by How the Event Ended*

	Number	Percentage
Use of force/assault	72	28.23
Show of force	63	24.70
Negotiation with inmates	55	21.56
Use of chemical agents	29	11.37
Voluntary surrender of inmates	24	9.41
Threats by prison administration	12	4.70
Totals	255	100%**

*Information on how the riot ended was not indicated in 1,079 riots
**The total may not equal 100 percent due to rounding.*

Impact of Prison Violence

Number of Inmates Involved

The range in the number of inmates involved in a prison riot from 1900 to 1995 varied from as few as 4 inmates to 65 occurrences having 500 or more involved, as shown in Figure 4.10. Of the 1,334 reported riots between 1900 and 1995, 821 supplied information about the number of inmates involved in the occurrence, but it was not supplied in 513 other occurrences.

A little over a fourth (28.13 percent or 231 reported incidents) of the violent occurrences that happened during this time period involved between twenty-five and forty-nine inmates. Only 135 incidents (16.44 percent) of the reported incidents involved between 15 and 24 inmates.

Figure 4.10 Distribution of American Prison Riots and Disturbances from 1900 to 1995 by Number of Inmates Involved*

	Number	Percentage
1 to 14 inmates	18	2.19
15 to 24 inmates	135	16.44
25 to 49 inmates	231	28.13
50 to 74 inmates	99	12.05
75 to 99 inmates	45	5.48
100 to 199 inmates	94	11.44
200 to 299 inmates	71	8.64
300 to 399 inmates	39	4.75
400 to 499 inmates	24	2.92
500 or more inmates	65	7.91
Totals	821	100%**

*The number involved was not reported in 513 riots
**The total may not equal 100 percent due to rounding.

Hostages

As Figure 4.11 shows the number of hostages taken during this ninety-five year period ranged from none to more than fifty. Fortunately, in almost three-fourths (264 or 71.54 percent) of the 1,334 reported incidents, no hostages were taken during the riot.

Figure 4.11. Distribution of American Prison Riots from 1900 to 1995 by Number of Hostages*

	Number	Percentage
0 hostages	264	71.54
1 to 5 hostages	62	16.80
6 to 10 hostages	19	5.14
11 to 20 hostages	14	3.79
21 to 49 hostages	7	1.89
50 or more hostages	3	.81
Totals	369	100%**

*Information on hostages was not reported in 965 incidents.
**The total may not equal 100 percent due to rounding.

However, information on hostages was not reported in 965 incidents. It is important to note that in sixty-two (16.80 percent) of these riots involving hostages, between one and five hostages were taken. These numbers must be considered with some caution in that of the 1,334 reported riots, hostage information was provided in only 369 reports.

Property Damage

Between 1900 and 1995, of the reported 1,334 prison riots and disturbances, the amount of property damage was not reported in 990 of the incidents. Using the remaining 344 occurrences, Figure 4.12 represents a breakdown of the distribution in the amount of property damage incurred after a prison riot.

Figure 4.12 Distribution of American Prison Riots and Disturbances 1990-1995 by Property Damage, Shown in Dollars*

	Number	Percentage
0	99	28.77
Less than 500	41	11.91
500 to 999	2	.58
1,000 to 4,999	26	7.55
5,000 to 9,999	8	2.32
10,000 to 14,999	17	4.94
15,000 to 19,999	1	.29
20,000 to 24,999	4	1.16
25,000 to 49,999	11	3.19
50,000 to 99,999	13	3.77
100,000 to 499,999	33	9.59
500,000 to 999,999	5	1.45
1 Million and over	21	6.10
Unspecified amount	63	18.31
Totals	344	100%**

Property damage was not reported in 990 incidents.
**The total may not equal 100 percent due to rounding.*

In ninety-nine (28.77 percent) of the reported occurrences, there was no notable property damage reported. In slightly less than half of this number (41 or 11.91 percent) the damage reported was less than $500. In 63 occurrences (18.31 percent) "unspecified amounts" of damage occurred. However, 21 (6.10 percent) of these riots resulted in property damage of $1 million or more.

Conclusion

While the previous figures allow some insight into "riot causation," there also must be some consideration of factors that are not represented effectively by this type of sampling. The issue of crowding is one area that does not seem to have received proper attention in the examination of reported causes of riots and disturbances from 1900 to 1995. Certainly, crowded conditions at least exacerbate all other problems in an institution. There are also issues concerning the architecture of prison buildings and the impact that it has on inmates. For example, many of the institutions designed for unit management have fewer violent incidents than those in linear facilities. Budgeting is another factor that will continue to require attention as mandatory sentencing fills American prisons to 200 and 300 percent of their maximum capacity.

There are many questions that come from this examination of prison riots and disturbances in America. For example, should inmates be divided by severity and type of offenses or by information from diagnostic testing that occurs in the processing once an inmate is incarcerated? Some feel that this area needs to be examined further to allow better security and possibly less inmate friction. There also will be continued issues about the lack of training of correctional officers and the role this has in riots and their severity.

Security issues were only 3.4 percent of the reported underlying causes of prison violence over this ninety-five years. However, do security measures (such as locked gates, personnel stations attended, inmate transfer procedures being followed, and so forth) have an impact on riots? Most administrators agree that these issues are vitally important. With respect to stopping occurrences once they begin and regaining control of an institution, one must inquire whether a "response team" is located on sight or available at all times, if there is proper coordination of efforts, and if so, if there are trained personnel or recruited employees available.

Of the approximately 1,334 riots and disturbances that have been reported in the United States from 1900 to 1995, the number one reported cause seems to be confrontations between inmates. Confrontations with other inmates was listed as the major reported cause of 399 violent occurrences between 1900 and 1995. This amounted to almost 30 percent of the reported sample. Most of the reported riots took place in the month of December. The states with the highest number of reported occurrences were California, Texas, Florida, New York, and Georgia.

Many experts feel effective administration is the key to prison-violence prevention. Dr. Bert Useem, noted expert in correctional violence research, sums up this philosophy well with the following statement: "When they break our rules, we punish them. When we break their rules, they punish us" (1991, p. 231).

The purpose of this chapter was to present a historical overview of prison violence in America. Data was collected on all reported prison riots during the last ninety-five years. Through this analysis, the authors hope the reader can understand the complexity of prison riots and their causes.

Theories of the Causes of Prison Violence

Introduction

While the previous discussions concerning the precipitating causes or "triggering events" of prison riots may provide insight to those who report violence or affect policy, such information is limited. Using this approach alone limits the possible insights that readers might gain from a study of prison riots, because a riot cannot be attributed to a single variable in the environment. The authors contend that riots cannot be understood solely by either underlying causes or "triggering events" alone. Because riots always involve multiple causes, consideration of theory is imperative.

> *"Attica is every prison; and every prison is Attica."*
>
> The Official Report of the New York State Special Commission on Attica, 1972

There is a distinction between the "triggering event(s)" of a riot and the cause of that riot. The underlying causes are the base from which the motivation or momentum of a riot originates. These factors then become actuated by a "triggering event." Such triggering events play an important role in justifying the ensuing violence from the viewpoint of the prisoners; however, the triggering event alone is not the single cause that generates the resulting violence.

Throughout the history and development of criminology, many theories have tried to explain the significant social variables that raise the probability of a prison riot. Many of these riot theories are founded on the exchange of power between the actors in the institution; other theories deal primarily with the expectations of the inmates. Some of the theories identify and explain "structured" or premeditated riot events, while others are attempts to understand "spontaneous" occurrences.

The purpose of this chapter is to review the basic concepts and principles of prison riot theories and to evaluate their adequacy and their applicability to America's penal institutions. The authors examine the dominant theories that have been employed to explain prison riots and categorize them into several major typologies. While this organization is not entirely chronological, it reflects the time periods in which each theory/typology was dominant in the literature on the subject. These ideas are categorized in Figure 5.1.

Figure 5.1. Principal Theories of Riots

Theory	Systems Theory
Assumptions	Prisons have difficulty accepting/integrating feedback
	Changes based on feedback produce institutional stress
	Custodial control alone also increases institutional stress
Insights	First attempt to explain riot causation
	Forms the foundation for numerous subsequent theories
Limitations	Reveals no significant variables for assessment
Contributing Researcher	Gresham Sykes, 1958
Theory	Environmental Conditions Theory
Assumptions	Factors are beyond the control of prison officials
Insights	Identifies contributing factors in riot causation (such as poorly trained staff, public indifference, and so forth)
Limitations	Does not provide any level of significance to variables
Contributing Researchers	Gresham Sykes, 1958; Randy Martin and Sherwood Zimmerman, 1990
Theory	Spontaneity (Powder Keg) Theory
Assumptions	Riots are spontaneous
	Riots are precipitated by abusive and/or oppressive circumstances
Insights	Reveals specific variables involved in riot causation (such as rumors, poor food, and so forth)
Limitations	Fails to explain riots that are premeditated and/or deliberate
Contributing Researchers	Gresham Sykes, 1958; R. Conant, 1968; Vernon Fox, 1971, 1972; R. Desroches, 1983; Susan Mahan, 1985

Theory	**Relative Deprivation/Rising-expectations Theory**
Assumptions	Collective violence is more probable when advancement is suspended after a cycle of progress There is a breach between the factual conditions of prison and the prisoner's perception
Insights	Displays the capacity that outside actors play in producing expectations
Limitations	Does not explain how expectations develop or start prison riots
Contributing Researchers	R. Conant, 1968; Richard A. Cloward, 1969; J. C. Davies, 1972; T. R. Gurr, 1972; R. Desroches, 1974; E. Flynn, 1980
Theory	**Conflict Theory**
Assumptions	Prison riots are a result of unresolved conflict There are two possible conditions that produce riots: subculture conflict and limited alternatives because of the prison environment
Insights	Identifies responses to conflict declaration Reveals significance of interactions between the actors involved
Limitations	Does not account for contributions made by casual actors
Contributing Researchers	R. Conant, 1968; Emerson Smith, 1973; Albert K. Cohan, 1976; Randy Martin and Sherwood Zimmerman, 1990
Theory	**Collective Behavior and Social Control**
Assumptions	Collective violence occurs in response to ungratified demands Prisons offer no valid outlets for complaint Authority in a penal institution is based on a system of social relationships
Insights	Identifies specific conditions in a specific order Identifies importance of mutual understanding of actors' roles
Limitations	Disregards impromptu riots
Contributing Researchers	Donald Clemmer, 1940; F. Hartung and M. Floch, 1957; N. J. Smelser, 1963, 1973; R. Conant, 1968; Vernon Fox, 1972; R. Gould, 1974; E. Stotland, 1976; B. Crouch, 1980; J. Irwin, 1980; E. Flynn, 1980; Susan Mahan, 1985; J. J. Dilulio, 1987; Todd Clear and George F. Cole, 1990; Randy Martin and Sherwood Zimmerman, 1990
Theory	**Time Bomb Theory**
Assumptions	Certain conditions must initially exist Riot is produced by spontaneous events
Insights	Reveals specific variables involved in riot causation (such as inmate confrontations, security issues, and so forth)

Limitations	Fails to explain riots that are premeditated and/or deliberate
Contributing Researcher	Vernon Fox, 1971
Theory	**Power Vacuum Theory**
Assumptions	Sudden reorganization can affect the security of a system
	Inmates exploit the gaps in a system under reorganization
Insights	Administration goal-hopping often disrupts the balance of power
Limitations	Fails to recognize the significance of environmental factors
	Does not address impulsively or unpremeditated riots
Contributing Researchers	Vernon Fox, 1971; R. Desroches, 1974; Barak-Glantz, 1982, 1985; Randy Martin and Sherwood Zimmerman, 1990
Theory	**Grievance Theory (Anomie)**
Assumptions	Suggests that prison riots are preplanned
	Legitimate opportunity to achieve goals is not available
	Riots are fueled by high levels of emotion
Insights	Identifies abrupt changes in institutional environment as significant to the instigation of prison riots
Limitations	Reveals no significant variables for assessment
Contributing Researchers	Emile Durkheim, 1897; Robert K. Merton, 1938; F.J. Desroches, 1983
Theory	**Theory of Riot Prevention**
Assumptions	Inmates are motivated to participate
Insights	Discusses significance of hope/positive motivation for prisoners
	Reveals importance of communication/diffusion practices
Limitations	Fails to discuss any significant variables
	Makes no distinctions between planned and spontaneous riots
Contributing Researchers	Michael Braswell, Steve Dillingham and Reid Montgomery, 1985
Theory	**Theory of Prison Riot Causation**
Assumptions	Specific pathology is evident
	Riot is produced because of the disorganization of the state
Insights	Identifies stages in a prison riot
	Identifies major elements essential for administrative breakdown
Limitations	Significance of labeled variables is not accessible for empirical measurement, rather they only are accessible through qualitative methodology
	Specific suggestions are not provided
Contributing Researchers	Bert Useem and Peter Kimball, 1991

Systems Theory

Gresham Sykes (1958) pioneered the first paradigm of a systems theory. He explained the preconditions that generated institutional riots. Sykes held that prisons were the type of organizations that had great difficulty in accepting and/or integrating new ideas or information, even if such information had originated from within the institution. "Outside" suggestions also were highly suspect as administrations generally were resistant to change. Because any new ideology usually generated a strain on the systematic maintenance of an already established prison system, recommendations typically were neglected or completely denied.

Sykes stated that the "strain" produced by such "feedback changes" usually was diverted into an ever-tightening loop or cycle that continued to constrict in its intensity. This level of increasing intensity eventually would cause the prison to reach a breaking point: the prison riot. The problem with this model arises because the avoidance of "strain" results in avoiding outside input whenever possible, in favor of making "custodial decisions" (generally very authoritative decisions with no input). These decisions, however, generated a similar dilemma in that they typically were effective only in the short run and failed to address underlying issues or problems.

Ironically, Sykes hypothesized that any type of managerial strategy that relied too heavily on "custodial decisions" also increased anxiety between the inmates and the control agents. Once again, this construct produces a climate in which violent incidents are more probable. When such an atmosphere had been established, an increase in momentum would follow, and eventually, the system would reach a point of critical mass. Following this massive build up of tension, a "spark" (some chance happening) then would occur and produce an emotional energy surge within the prison population. Because this populace already was predisposed to collective violence, the prison riot would ensue.

This initial theory of Sykes serves as the basis for many current theories. While this model produced breakthroughs for the study of institutional violence, it did not produce independent significant variables by which to assess prison riots. To explain prison riots, researchers need additional perspectives.

Environmental Conditions Theory

When asked to rationalize why prison riots have occurred, many correctional administrators allude to the environmental conditions of the institution as the primary cause. The environmental conditions theory (Martin and Zimmerman, 1990) accounts for the contributing factors in the architectural environment, and the resources within a prison setting that may contribute to a riot. Significant examples of such variables found throughout criminology literature include the following: inferior quality or amount of food, crowding, inadequate staff, poorly trained staff, cruelty, public indifference, inhumane administration, gross neglect, habitual indolence of correctional officers toward inmates, and lack of/or inadequate treatment programs.

Some institutional administrators consider these factors as beyond their control, either due to a lack of resources or conflicting political agendas. This explanation reduces the responsibility of those directly accountable. While it is a safe stance for administrators to assume in the aftermath of a riot, the reasoning behind it is often inadequate.

Yet, many of these environmental conditions are present in institutions that had experienced riots, and such variables indeed may have played a role; nevertheless, this model does not reveal any level of significance to support such variables. For example, while it is evident that many of these factors exist in prisons that have seen riots, many more prisons suffer from the same conditions, yet had no prison riots. Therefore, while these variables may have been essential for a prison riot to occur, they clearly were not an adequate foundation for predicting riots. Thus, while the environmental conditions theory provides some insight into certain preconditions that had a strong correlation with institutional riots, it did not explain the reason for such violence.

Time Bomb/Spontaneity/Powder Keg Theories

Dr. Vernon Fox (1971), a noted criminologist, theorized that prison riots were actually spontaneous, and accordingly, he developed the time bomb theory. When certain conditions (for example, extremely punitive administrative control, crowding, high turnover rates, low inmate morale, and so forth) exist, the prisons become ticking time bombs. Such potentially destructive institutions typically were detonated by spontaneous events. The theory is composed of five separate stages. Four of these stages occurred during the riot itself, with the fifth stage immediately following the riot.

> First, there is a period of undirected violence like an exploding bomb. Second, inmate leaders tend to emerge and organize around themselves a group of ringleaders who determine inmate policy during the riot. Third, a period of interaction with prison authority, whether by negotiation or by force, assists in identifying the alternatives available for the resolution of the riot. Fourth, the surrender of the inmates, whether by negotiation or by force, phases out the violent event. Fifth, and more important from the political viewpoint, the investigations and administrative changes restore order and confidence in the remaining power structure by making "constructive changes" to regain

administrative control and to rectify the undesirable situation that produced a riot (Fox, 1971, p.9).

Fox's theory (1972) allowed insight into the collective actions of the inmates and administration involved in a prison riot. The metaphor of a prison a time bomb or powder keg served the researcher well, as certain significant conditions concerning oppressive and abusive (physical assaults, emotional torment, and so forth) prison characteristics (lack of privacy, denial of civil rights, and so forth) and variables were discovered. By exploring such variables, changes may be possible within prison institutions to deter violent collective behaviors. However, the time bomb and spontaneity theory failed to explain premeditated riots.

Another theory, the Spontaneity (Powder Keg) Theory (Desroches, 1983) attempted to refine and extend Fox's convictions. It presented the notion that prison riots generally occurred in a spontaneous fashion, but such institutional outbursts systematically were precipitated by abusive and/or oppressive circumstances.

Relative Deprivation/ Rising-expectations Theory

Davies (1972) developed the model of relative deprivation. He postulated that collective violence was more probable when improvements had slowed down or were suspended in a prison after a cycle of expansion, upgrades, or improvement. Closely related to this is the rising-expectations theory, which suggests a breach exists between the actual conditions of the prison and the prisoner's perception of what institutional life was or should have been (Gurr, 1972). Various social scientists have employed the relative deprivation and the rising-expectations paradigms to isolate relevant variables in prison riot scenarios.

Desroches (1974) used a variation of these theories as he reviewed common dilemmas that tended to occur after prison authorities had increased security within an institution. These augmentations to prison security typically followed periods when high levels of discretion had been practiced. Because of such periods of discretion, infractions had come to be justifiable and expected. The inmates' expectations were different than the conditions realized after the security increased, and as a result, attempts to change the existing factors of the institutions produced the "breach" between reality and expectation of the inmates.

The relative deprivation/rising-expectations models (Davies, 1972) highlighted the capacity that institutional administrators, coalitions, and organizations have had with respect to building greater expectations in the minds of the inmate populations. While this theory has allowed researchers to examine the influence that actors exterior to the penal institution may have played, it is insufficient to illustrate or explain what develops expectations or what significant roles such expectations play in generating prison riots.

Conflict Theory

The conflict theory model (Martin and Zimmerman, 1990) is centered on the restraining-authority system that is used in prison and its impact on such institutional settings. This theory also examines the subculture friction produced by employing this managerial strategy, as well as the inmates' limited alternatives in responding to this type of control. The conflict model is grounded on the premise that two feasible conditions advance the possibility of an institutional riot: the production of subculture conflict, and limited alternatives for reaction due to the physical environment.

Emerson A. Smith (1973) developed the conflict theory of riots. Smith believed that prison riots resulted from unresolved conflicts. Conflict existed, according to Smith, when one actor desired another to exercise a level of power in a specified manner. However, the other actor involved—for whatever reason—did not exercise this type and/or direction of power. Smith stated that accompanying this disagreement in how to exercise power was typically a conflict declaration, which was a verbal or written specification stating how the initial actor expected the other to exercise some level of power.

According to Smith, four possible reactions to a conflict declaration, or a possible riot, were the following (1) the participants may bargain with each other, (2) one participant may withdraw from the conflict, (3) the participants may engage in physical combat, or (4) a third party may be called in to mediate the conflict. One or more of the anticipated reactions discussed in this model may occur at different points throughout the life of a prison riot.

A famous example of this occurred in the 1971 Attica riot. This riot, when viewed through the conflict model, would have departed from Smith's definition in that it included several of the conflict model's possible reactions to a "conflict declaration" (such as bargaining, mediation, and finally physical combat). Initially, there was bargaining among the prisoners and the administration (Oswald and the inmate leaders). Next, a group of third-party observers were brought in to help resolve the riot. And finally, the state used force to retake the institution and end the riot.

This theory advanced the notion that conflict within a prison setting was likely because of the very nature of a prison in relation to its inmates. When an adverse condition arose, the inmates did not have the option of evading it. Also, inmates frequently resorted to violence as the only recognized alternative to achieving their desired goal of change. While this was not as prevalent a choice for most social groups, inmates were unique because they had few options due to their physical confinement.

The conflict theory's attempt to explore the cause of prison riots revealed much concerning the interactions between the actors involved (inmates and prison social-control agents). This description, however, did not consider contributions made by more casual actors (such as politicians and local civil authorities) and the level of public support, which also may have influenced control within a prison setting. Interaction between these less formal actors and others already discussed in many cases often has been influential in determining the level of probable conflict within a prison.

Collective Behavior and Social Control Theory

Collective violence regularly has been generated by people and the institutions that they have created. Individuals or groups seeking to seize, maintain, or regain the elements of power continually have engaged in collective violence as part of their campaigns. Justification for such action typically depended on the perspective of the attacker: the oppressed crying out for justice, the advantaged calling for order, and those caught in the middle acting out of fear, but all believing their actions to be just. Conant (1968) and Flynn (1980) concurred that collective violence, especially in the form of prison riots, was perhaps the ultimate response from the collective mass over ungratified demands. Collective violence as a phenomenon often has caused great shifts of power to take place within groups, organizations, institutions, and even nations of the world. Of course, the form that each of these acts has taken is quite dependent on both who was involved and the motivation or issue at hand.

The nature of collective violence and the character of society often have been highly akin (such as the collective behavior of the inmates during the Attica riot in 1971). However, the attributes of such violence were not always desired by the societies that they served, nor were these occurrences always avoidable. Because prisons are a mirror of the society in which they occur, by careful observation of the persistence of collective violence, the levels of intensity at which it operates, and the changes in its form over time, we are better able to understand the contemporary styles of prison protest.

A dramatic American example of such undesirable reactions to collective movements occurred in the civil rights movement of the late 1960s. In response to public demand for law enforcement accountability, in 1968, President Lyndon B. Johnson established the *President's Commission on Law Enforcement and the Administration of Justice*. The Commission was charged with determining what "caused" the public unrest in the nation, and what the possible "solutions" were to this problem. The final response of this commission was that "disorganization in society and in law enforcement" was the major cause of public unrest. The Commission determined that additional monies and research were needed in the criminal justice system for it to adjust to the quickly changing society it serves.

Many unique aspects of our society and politics have contributed to the individual and collective violence that has troubled contemporary American prisons. Smelser (1963) proclaimed, in his collective behavior theory, a unique approach to understanding collective behavior. He identified specific conditions in a specific sequence, all of which must be present that increase the probability of a riot. There are six such conditions or determinants of a riot.

(1) Structural conduciveness (such as age and physical condition of institution, inadequate spacing, and other issues)

(2) Strain or tension (such as quality of institutional life, administrative inattention, and other issues)

(3) Growth or spread of a generalized belief (such as misinformation, formation of prison subculture, and other issues)

(4) Precipitation factors (such as conflict between staff and inmates, racial conflicts, and other issues)

(5) Mobilization and organization for action (such as inmate leaders, inadequate grievance process, and other issues)

(6) Operation of mechanisms of social control (such as perception of administrative authority, effectiveness of authoritative deterrence, level of staffing, and so forth)

In 1972, Dr. Vernon Fox held that society, in general, provided many outlets for public complaints, most obviously the legal system. However, when these processes and structures were no longer symbiotic with the public's needs, collective responses became much more probable.

I. L. Barak-Glantz (1982) stated that the principal application of authority in a penal institution was not accomplished by force, but rather through the means of a complex social system of relationships. The direct and indirect coercion of these formal and informal actors (respectively) in the prison environment produced a level of cooperative control. In other words, positive institutional control was obtained by agreement, and by participation of the prisoners (Irwin, 1980).

To achieve the required agreement, both inmates and administration had to maintain the institutional balance. To do this, the actors in the prison setting construct unofficial understandings. Anything that disrupts these interrelationships becomes a potential threat to the delicate balance of control (Martin and Zimmerman, 1990). Disruptions may range from inmate complacency to collective violence.

When considering the collective behavior/social control perspective, Martin and Zimmerman (1990) discovered that maintaining positive administrative control over a prison for a long period of time was only possible when there was some mutual understanding of the roles played by each institutional actor. This defied the common myth that the application of custodial force alone was not functional in a long-term prison setting. From the perspective of this model, the probability of a riot occurring significantly increased when the formal and informal system of social relationships was disrupted or collapsed (Gould, 1974; Flynn, 1980; Irwin, 1980; Mahan, 1985; and DiIulio, 1987).

The collective behavior and social control paradigms centered around the relationships (both formal and informal) that were necessary for the control in an institutional setting. Many significant variables are required to establish the conditions necessary for an institution to preserve a safe balance of power. However, while these theories directed their attention to the roles played by the institutional actors, they tended to disregard riots generated in unpremeditated fashion.

Power Vacuum Theory

The power vacuum theory (Barak-Glantz, 1982) considered the effects that sudden and consequential reorganization could have on the formal command system within a prison setting. Such attempts at reorganization often generated divisions or crevices in the formal control used to coordinate administrative command over an institution. Inmates, in turn, attacked these gaps in the system in an attempt to exploit it.

Within any organizational system, there are sets of goals, objectives, and controls, which are formalized and coordinated over time. Whenever a reorganization of these factors is undertaken, by new or old administrative leadership, the administration must realign its goals. Any lack of communication or coordination during the reorganization period may create confusion, on which the inmates may capitalize. When an institution enters such a state, or when some level of inadequacy or ineffectualness on the part of the state exists, this is referred to as a "power vacuum" (Martin and Zimmerman, 1990).

Dr. Vernon Fox (1971) held that the current trend of prison administration goal-hopping from the systematic view of the "custody philosophy" to that of a "rehabilitative ideology" often distorts the balance of control within a prison. Such a shift in ideology creates an imbalance between regulating and developing tenants within an institution (in other words, which philosophy and practice is ultimately used—rehabilitation or incapacitation). As a result, conflicts in the form of open rebellion may develop between institutional workers and prison authorities. Fox stated that such circumstances were highly instrumental in generating collective disorder and violence. Prisoners often will see themselves as either pawns or victims in many "pendulum-style" prison management systems, and will react accordingly (such as through riots, work stoppage, food strikes, and refusal to submit to authority).

The power-vacuum perspective explored the contribution that goal modification, or the disturbance of the present institutional balance, could have on prison rebellion. While researchers and practitioners gained insight

There are often cases when an institution's doctrine is challenged by the courts or other civil authorities, and thus the accompanying tactics that are in place also come under attack. When these types of scenarios are presented to a penal institution, it can produce negative fall-out among the prisoners who are subject to the tactics, policies, and regulations in question.

A law in the State of New York stated that jail prisoners (classified as pretrial detainees) could not accumulate their time spent in jail before a guilty judgment (if found guilty and sentenced to serve time) to be utilized later when analyzing their prison "good-time credits." A court of appeals ruled the code to be unconstitutional; however, the state government appealed this decision. The Supreme Court heard the case and reversed the appellate court's ruling, stating that the New York law disallowing particular state prisoners "good-time credit" toward their parole qualification for the term of their presentence jailing does not infringe on the equal protection clause of the Fourteenth Amendment. *McGinnis v. Royster*, 410 U.S. 263, 93 S.Ct. 1055 (1972).

into the problems that the reorganization of goals/objectives could have on an institution's current authority system, this model failed to recognize or credit the significance that circumstances and environmental factors could play on the probability of a prison riot. This theory also did not address riots that were generated impulsively or in an unpremeditated fashion.

Grievance Theory (Anomie)

Contradictory to the ideology of the spontaneity theory, the grievance theory (Desroches, 1983) suggests that prison riots are premeditated, and such acts of violence are calculated and rational. These occurrences are frequently attempts to obtain specific goals.

Prior to this, in 1938, Merton (Desroches, 1983) suggested a similar theory known as "anomie." Anomie occurs within a socially structured interaction, in which certain groups endeavor to obtain socially approved goals. They discover, however, that legitimate opportunities to achieve these goals are not available, are obstructed, or simply do not exist. The anomie theory as offered by Durkheim in 1897 implied that prison riots were fueled much differently. Durkheim suggested that these acts were generated by a high level of emotion and that this type of reaction generally resulted from a form of moral indignation. In other words, an expressive mechanism that released frustration engendered by a sense of powerlessness was the initial motivation for violence. In both cases, the inmates' motivations produced violence, which according to the grievance theory, is then directed at achieving a specific goal.

An example in which the grievance theory may be applicable occurred at a state prison system (Broad River Correctional Institution, Columbia, South Carolina), when a newly appointed commissioner implemented different regulations for the inmate population concerning acceptable hair-length. This abrupt change resulted in an inmate rebellion that escalated into a riot. This type of violence, as viewed through the grievance model, may have been avoidable if this new policy had been introduced over a longer period of time, allowing for a smoother transition.

When considering the implementation of institutional changes, subscription to these theories would warrant that a specific effort be made to avoid deregulating values and procedures within the institution. This would be achieved best by introducing any changes in technique, policy, or program in a way that maintains institutional stability. Simply put, the grievance theory suggests that reforms should be introduced carefully and at a regulated rate.

Theory of Riot Prevention

Dr. Ellis MacDougall (Braswell, Dillingham, and Montgomery, 1985) held that the best way to prevent a prison riot was to provide "hope" for inmates. A key element in this process included good communication between the inmates and the administration. Prison administrators who communicated with their entire organization and regularly dealt with emerging problems were more likely to avoid prison disturbances through early detection and diffusion practices.

Another method of providing hope for inmates was "positive motivation." MacDougall stated that the effective warden would develop programs that promoted positive attitudes. With these practices in place, it was possible to identify disgruntled inmates and prevent them from influencing others. "Participatory management" could help to increase the level of hope for inmates. MacDougall felt that it was essential for inmates and employees to feel that they had a voice in their institution's management process. The theory proposed that people who were allowed to participate in management decisions would take more active roles within the organization. Individuals who did not feel a part of the organization would be more likely to criticize and work against such systems.

MacDougall (Braswell, Dillingham, and Montgomery, 1985) believed that prisons populated by violent individuals who lack productive activities or programs and who are devoid of hope posed serious threats to institutional safety and tranquility. An inmate with no hope had nothing to lose by rioting. While this perspective provided an understanding of the motivational factors that could be used in riot-prevention efforts, it failed to discuss any significant variables. This theory also made no distinctions between planned and spontaneous riots, or prevention strategies that might have been applicable.

Theory of Prison Riot Causation

Dr. Bert Useem and Dr. Peter Kimball (1991) believed that from the time a prison riot ensued until it was fully developed, a certain pathology was evident. The prisoners' ability to seize some level of control over the institution always was attributed to the "disorganization of the state rather than to the organization of the inmates." Useem and Kimball have defined a prison riot in the following manner, "A prison riot occurs when the authorities lose control of a significant number of prisoners, in a significant area of the prison, for a significant amount of time" (p.4).

They divided a prison riot into five stages. The first of these stages was distinguished as the "pre-riot" state. In this period preceding the riot, prisoners and the forces of the state developed materials and cognitive resources to significantly determine the course of the event. During the second stage, the "initiation stage," an action on the part of the inmates initiates an open rebellion. This period includes the initial response of the state to the rebellious act.

Assuming the disturbance was not immediately quashed, and full control of the institution was not reestablished by the state, the third stage would begin. During this "expansion" stage, the prisoners attempt to gain control of as many resources as possible, including material, human, and spatial resources. This is done to counter the resistance or nonresistance of the state with respect to the newly formed riot (Useem and Kimball, 1991).

Stage four, known as the "state of siege" generally follows. This stage of the riot was typically more stable in its makeup because the prisoners maintained some control of the territory within the institution. This stage often resembles a battle in which the lines of control have been established. During this time, the state also assessed its resources by assembling counterforces and considering the possible options for retaking control of the prison. This stage may include bargaining between the state and the prisoners or mediating parties; however, this is not necessarily the case. The last stage of a riot, according to Useem and Kimball is "termination" or "recapture" of the prison. During this time, the state once again assumes control of the previously rioting institution.

Useem and Kimball (1991) believed that a major factor concerning riots was a "breakdown in administrative control and operation of the prison." Major elements of such a breakdown included factors such as scandals, public dissent among correctional actors, and problems from outsiders coming into the system.

According to Useem and Kimball (1991), another major factor in prison riot causation was the "erosion of the security system." Erosion of a prison's security system made it more probable that inmates would initiate disturbances. However, it also made it more likely that such a disturbance would expand into a full-scale riot. Properly followed, security measures such as locked and maintained security grills, as well as swift adherence to disturbance procedures, would demonstrate the confident mobilization and prepared force that a state was willing to take to maintain dominant control over an institution. With such operating procedures in place, any incident that was not sufficiently deterred would have been shorter in its overall duration, if not prevented from spreading.

Quick, quality administration is the key to preventing prison riots (Useem and Kimball, 1991). Good administration provides work, adequate cell space, proper programming, and the amenities of life that meet a reasonably legitimate standard.

Many theories have attempted to explain the increases in prison violence in recent decades. Porporino (1986) stated that overcrowding affects the physical and psychological well-being of inmates and appears to lead to more violence through destabilization of inmate social networks. Data derived from nineteen prisons operated by the federal government showed that assaults increased with overcrowding (Gaes and McGuire, 1985). These security issues often result in a breakdown in administrative control and operations in an institution.

Factors exacerbating the increase in the state prison populations between 1985 and 1995 involve:

- A 91 percent rise in the number of admissions from 1985 to 1990 and a 13 percent rise from 1990 to 1995

- A decline in annual release rates of prisoners from 37 percent in 1990 to 31 percent in 1995

- A sharp rise in violent offenders among white inmates (accounting for 42 percent of the ten-year increase in white prisoners) and in drug offenders among black inmates (42 percent of their increase)

(Bureau of Justice Statistics, June 1997)

The physical conditions of an institution are a large factor in the overall security and quality of life that its inmates experience. One of the most cited reasons for poor quality of life within a prison or jail has been crowded conditions. The building of new prisons has become a race between the rate at which they can be built and the continually expanding United States prison population.

The capacity of an institution is often difficult to determine as various measures can be used by different institutions. This absence of uniform measures makes an accurate estimation of overall crowding in American prisons problematic. Some of these capacity measures are developed by considering available space to house prisoners while others are rooted in the staffing and operation of an institution. Three typical measures include rated, operational, and design capacities. These methods for measuring crowding are defined as follows:

- *Rated capacity* is the number of beds or inmates assigned by a rating official to institutions within the jurisdiction

- *Operational capacity* is the number of inmates that can be provided for based on a facility's staff, existing programs, and services

- *Design capacity* is the total number of prisoners that developers or architects calculated for the facility to house

(Bureau of Justice Statistics, June 1997)

Modifications to Causation

The causes of a riot, as discussed previously, often evolve as inmates move toward the point where a triggering event and its consequences can occur. Individuals can develop a more in-depth understanding of these modifications to the original cause when considering the many contingencies or outside circumstances. These modifications would include, but are not limited to: (1) the staff and inmate perceptions, (2) the effectiveness of leadership, (3) the various rationales that motivate the inmates to rebel, (4) the prison culture and strengths of accompanying institutional ideologies, (5) the use or abuse of alcohol or other drugs, (6) factors in the architectural environment, (7) the response of officials and staff to the potential problem, (8) the past effects of the media, (9) and information inmates receive about the current state of affairs.

Modification of the original cause can be detected in nearly any kind of incident. A common example of this might occur when inquiring about racial tension and the disturbances it often creates within a prison setting. Racial tension would be viewed in this case as a precipitating event or "triggering" device, by which an underlying cause was able to manifest itself. To reach an understanding of the fundamental source of the problem, certain questions must be asked. These questions would include (1) Why does the racial strain exist? (2) What managerial or administrative procedures or policies have contributed to it? (3) Has the demographic nature of the staff and/or inmate population contributed to the tension? (4) Have external individuals played a part in instigating or promoting the tension? (5) What has been the contribution of inmate hate groups?

> In 1974, a Prisoners' Labor Union was organized within a state prison for several purposes including a venue in which to address prison conditions, grievance for inmates, and other tasks of interest to the inmates. Eventually, this labor union was deemed problematic by institutional officials, and, as a result, many of its activities were curtailed. The union brought a lawsuit against the institution grounded in an appeal for the right to request the participation of other prisoners in their union through bulk mailings and informative meetings. The Supreme Court found in favor of the North Carolina prison administrators and stated that a prohibition on inmate union activities is not a violation of the First Amendment (right to free speech and assembly), nor is it in violation of the Fourteenth Amendment (right for equal protection and due process). *Jones v. North Carolina Prisoners' Labor Union*, Inc., 433 U.S. 119, 97 S.Ct. 2532 (1977).

Such questions reaffirm the complexity of interactions that lead to a riot, and suggest that riots indeed never stem from a single cause. Only by fully examining various causation factors can we develop an understanding of the sources and triggering events that lead to prison violence. Then, based on this, we will be able to develop appropriate social and administrative policies to prevent or limit such occurrences.

A prison's social environment can, and often does, generate a subculture which is shared to a different extent by each individual. However, when one concept or ideology is dominantly shared among the inmates (often involving more than one prison), a "movement" may emerge. Such activities have produced changes resulting in various outcomes, ranging from prison labor unions to court orders that mandate the revamping of institutional policies. This collective effort, fueled by a subculture or ideology, has been significant in shaping America's penal institutions.

A 1977 case in North Carolina was brought by inmates stating that they were being denied equal protection and just access to the courts. The inmates founded their accusations in the fact that they were not provided with adequate law library facilities. In response to the complaints, prison officials proposed the creation of seven libraries throughout the state to serve the inmate populations. However, the Supreme Court held that this offer would not be sufficient because each prison would not be individually served, and instead, alternative forms of legal assistance would be offered to the inmates. Such assistance could be offered in the form of paralegals, part-time and/or full-time on-site lawyers. This Supreme Court decision was consequential as it justified alternatives to law libraries as an acceptable means of inmate legal assistance. *Bounds v. Smith*, 430 U.S. 817, 97 S.Ct. 1491 (1977). Such a successful resolution of a problem probably lowered the tension in institutions and may have helped prevent a riot.

Conclusion

Prison riot theories involve the search for information to aid in both the making of prison policy and the maintaining of institutional security. The theories presented in this chapter are attempts to explain significant factors related to prison riots. These theories, as all others, may be evaluated by comparing them to other theories on the basis of the criteria of clarity and consistency, scope, testability, empirical validity, and the practical application that the information may have.

While none of the previously discussed theories fully explain the social phenomenon of prison riots or why they take place, their combined insights may offer some comprehensive understanding. In sum, these theories have attempted to explore and explain the environmental factors and other associations that are relevant. Although each model focuses on different aspects of prison riots, typically the models are compatible, as they are inclined to act as a complement or continuation of one another.

Analyzing the phenomenon of prison riots is often difficult because of the very nature of institutional riots. Penal riots occur only sporadically, and even at this rate, information in the past often has been difficult for the researcher to access. This was especially true before the Freedom of Information Acts became uniformly used through the United States. Because of this, information concerning riots usually is analyzed using secondary analysis and retrospective research. Such methodology produces little reliable and valid information, and is typically very limited. However, after examining the major paradigms of riot causation, we anticipate that the merits and weaknesses of each model will be more apparent, and that the readers will be able to apply the theories presented here more clearly when they examine prison riots.

Understanding Equals Deterrence

Introduction

Amerian prisons currently are bulging with inmates, and predictions are that, if the current trends of the 1990s continue, by the early twenty-first century, over 2 million individuals will be incarcerated in correctional institutions across the United States. In the mid-1990s, there were more offenders incarcerated per capita in the United States than in any other industrialized nation in the world (Silberman, 1995). This crowding historically has caused prisons to be extremely dangerous and often inhumane places.

> *"Communication, communication, communication . . . it can't just go one way, you have to listen to these people, too!"*
>
> Dr. Vernon Fox, when asked by the authors what he felt would be the most effective way to reduce the amount of prison violence being experienced in America, April 20, 1997

As a response to the looming problem of crowding, the federal and state governments have responded with an unprecedented rate of construction of new prison facilities. However, this effort would seem limited, as the anticipated level of the inmate population currently is beyond the scope that the construction of new prisons can address. The U.S. Justice Department notes that the number of inmates in the nation's jails and prisons has almost tripled in the last sixteen years, growing from half a million in 1980 to 1.5 million in 1996. During this same time period, the incarceration rate per 100,000 more than doubled from a rate of 221 in 1980 to 529 in 1993 (*Corrections Compendium*, April 1996). In 1995, 5.5 million people were on probation, in jail or prison, or on parole. This number was nearly 2.8 percent of the entire United States adult population. As Figure 6.1 shows, in 1996, state and federal prisons held about 1.2 million prisoners, and local jails held about 599,300 adults who were awaiting trial or serving a sentence (Bureau of Justice Statistics, 1997a).

Figure 6.1. Inmate Population Increases 1985-1995

	Number of Inmates		Sentenced Inmates per 100,000	
Year	Federal	State	Federal	State
1985	40,223	462,284	14	187
1990	65,526	708,393	20	272
1991	71,608	753,951	22	287
1992	80,259	802,241	26	305
1993	89,587	880,857	29	330
1994	95,034	959,668	30	356
1995	100,250	1,026,043	32	379
1996	105,544	1,076,625	33	394

Source: Bureau of Justice Statistics (June, 1997). *Prisoners in 1996.*

This exponential rate of growth is the result of the increased regulations that have been demanded by the American public of the 1990s. Anticrime legislation (including but not limited to, the enhancement of drug and weapon laws) has activated a chain of "get tough" policies that have had an impact on the American prison population. Other examples of this ideology include the "three strikes and you're out" and the "truth in sentencing" acts of this decade. These types of laws, while attempting to protect the moral fiber of society, tend to fill jails and prisons with a high number of nonviolent offenders. Perhaps modification of these policies regarding nonviolent offenders represents a place to begin in the search for a relief valve, in a system that is waiting to explode (*see also* Lauen, 1997).

The changing federal prison population is strongly associated with drug and weapon violations in the United States. Inmates sentenced for drug offenses constituted the single largest group of federal inmates (60 percent) in 1995, up from 34 percent in 1985. The increase of more than 42,000 drug offenders accounted for more than 80 percent of the total growth in federal inmates.

Since 1985, the number of Federal inmates serving time for weapon offenses has soared, from 926 inmates in 1985 to 7,519 in 1995. By year-end 1995, weapon offenders constituted the second largest group of federal inmates (Bureau of Justice Statistics, 1997a).

While tougher sentencing has become the standard for the federal government, many states and local legislatures seem to be following suit. An example of this shifting emphasis is demonstrated by several states adopting sentencing guidelines similar to those of the federal government. These reforms certainly will intensify rather than alleviate the problem surrounding prison populations. For example, Oregon expects its inmate population to increase by 102 percent over the next six years; Kentucky expects a 109 percent increase over the same

Crowded prison in South Carolina.
(*Source:* South Carolina State Archives)

period; and Mississippi expects an increase of 157 percent over current levels within the same time period (*Corrections Compendium*, April, 1996).

Because of this tougher sentencing, the growth in the number of prisoners has caused crowded conditions. An appellate court has ruled that the vast majority of the state prison systems are in violation of the Eighth Amendment prohibition against cruel and unusual treatment due to crowding combined with other harmful prison conditions. Although crowding alone has been determined as a reasonable consequence of a criminal conviction, crowding does not violate the Eighth Amendment unless other inhumane conditions also are present (Skovron, 1988).

Many of these issues do not directly concern the general public unless they see their taxes increase, become incarcerated, or have someone they know go to prison. Some reports predict that 5.1 percent of all Americans will be confined in a state or federal prison at some point during their lifetime. Demographically speaking, this rate is higher for men (9 percent) than it is for women (1.1 percent). It is significantly higher for blacks (16.2 percent) and Hispanics (9.4 percent) than it is for whites (2.5 percent) (Bureau of Justice Statistics, 1997a).

As crowding increases and more people become "involved" in corrections, either as inmates or as members of the ever-growing correctional employee population, there will be expanding interest in this area of American society. Hopefully, this increased interest will generate more involvement in efforts to determine the future directions of correctional reform. As the number of individuals becoming interested in corrections increases, so will the number of vantage points and opinions.

Chapter six provides an overview of some of the present practices and philosophies employed in correctional systems across the country. Also presented is an examination of various views on proper prison management and several futuristic approaches to be considered and/or developed for prison control techniques in the twenty-first century.

Reported Problems Inherent in Prisons in the 1990s

Figure 6.2 lists the dilemmas that are reported typically as problems inherent in modern prisons. Many feel that these problems are the cornerstones of any and all violence in America's prisons. Without considering and acting on these problem areas, there can be no realistic hope of lessening the number of prison riots or their potential for occurring.

Figure 6.2. Problems in Prisons

Crowding (inmate spacing)	Antiquated architecture
Inadequate budgeting	Poor facility management
Mandatory sentencing	Antiquated inmate classification
Poor security	Inherent inmate friction
Absence of proper staff training	Low staff pay
Lack of coordination of efforts	Lack of response teams
Public dissatisfaction	Lack of program resources
Inadequate staffing levels	Noise
Inability to coordinate mass movement	

Source: Bureau of Justice Statistics (June, 1997). Prisoners in 1996.

Correctional officers at Kirkland Correctional Institution, Columbia, South Carolina.
(*Source:* South Carolina Department of Corrections – Mr. Al Waters' Collection)

Characteristics of the Modern Inmate Population

The population profile of modern American correctional institutions is a major factor to be considered when examining the causes of prison riots. Yet, characteristics of the modern inmate population is a very basic factor that often is not considered when attempting to establish policy to deal with possible inmate unrest. When the present correctional population profile is examined, it is surprising that there are not many more violent incidents given the present lack of available resources on a day-to-day basis for correctional managers to use.

The vast majority of prisons in the United States mainly are populated by young, unmarried, minority males. The majority of these persons are also from a very low socioeconomic status. A very large percentage of these individuals are educationally deficient, emotionally unstable, and prone to violent or other socially unacceptable behavior. Many of these inmates have unstable work records, prior criminal histories, low self-esteem, and usually are products of broken homes. Most have no major goals in life and only measure personal success by material success. Many are manipulative, threatening, and antisocial (American Correctional Association, 1996). It is obvious that society has not been able to meet these individuals' needs, but very often correctional institutions are expected to do so.

Even with an inmate population such as this, most inmates still want to become responsible members of the institutional community once they are confined. Most generally want the institution to run smoothly and want their lives to be as pleasant and as safe as possible given their present circumstances. They realize that no one has more to lose in a riot than they do. They have the greatest risk of being injured or killed, having personal property stolen or destroyed, and having to deal with the long lockdown after a disturbance. Most inmates will want order restored and issues resolved quickly once a disturbance does begin, although a minority will want it to continue and escalate (Braswell, Montgomery, and Lombardo, 1994).

There are some special groups found in modern correctional institutions who, for a variety of reasons, will want violence to begin and will continue to incite others to be violent once a disturbance does occur. Some present inmates have an antisocial personality disorder—they are angry at society and want to "pay back" any and all with whom they come into contact for the "mistreatment" that they feel life has given them. There also continues to be a growing number of former mental patients in American correctional institutions. Very often these inmates actually can "trigger" a violent incident or general unrest in the inmate population. Other inmates, who have no idea how to deal with these persons, become frustrated in not being able to remove themselves from situations involving these individuals (Henderson, Rauch, and Phillips, 1997).

> In a correctional institution, there must be a division of work if inmates are to be guarded and fed, problems and paperwork attended to, and payroll maintained. However, because security and watchfulness are everyone's responsibilities, everyone should be familiar, at least to a certain extent, with several other tasks to be able to fill in during emergencies. In some systems, for example, riot plans call for secretaries to take position in certain gun towers to free correctional officers for more specialized and dangerous duties (James Houston, 1995).

Many inmates have significant histories of substance abuse. This, in itself, predisposes an inmate to certain types of behavior. The inmate may demonstrate aggressive or impulsive action patterns or become involved in prison gang membership for increased access to substances. Prison gang membership itself has continued to increase in the last several decades. Polarization of a correctional population continues to prompt individual acts of misconduct associated with gang activity, which contributes to a disturbance-prone situation (Miller and Rush, 1996).

Fortunately for correctional management, inmates do not often unite. This primarily is due to the historical fact that inmates generally have great difficulty sharing goals and objectives. Historically, it is common for an inmate leader to command a large following, but almost impossible to control an entire institution for any length of time. Inmate frustration is the strongest ally that inmate leaders can use to their advantage (Useem and Kimball, 1991).

Inmate leaders know that it is easier to agitate and convince others to join them in aggressive acts when there is already a high level of inmate frustration. As tension builds in an institution, a condition of emotional contagion often develops. Simple incidents become fertile grounds for a possibly violent encounter. Rumors often can run rampant and can cause small groups of dissatisfied inmates to become violent mobs. Often, these times can produce an unusual sense of psychological unity between inmates, while at the same time, they begin to lose their sense of self-discipline. When this occurs, a prison disturbance is only a small step away (Henderson, Rauch, and Phillips, 1997).

Staff Perceptions of Prison Problems

There is a strong body of knowledge regarding what significant factors contribute to tension, stress, and safety levels within a prison setting. These data pools, however, often contradict one another depending on what sources were used (who was interviewed and so forth). One such study was conducted by Knut Rostad and Leonard Witke (1997) and revealed what staff perceived to be contributing factors related to safety, assault, and housing unit control. As shown in Figure 6.3, the research revealed that staff believed that the most important issue associated with safety, assault, and control was inmate behavior. It also was interesting to note that "management techniques" were ranked as the least important of the discovered factors.

In Rostad and Witke's (1997) study, staff also were surveyed as to which factors contributed significantly to tension and stress within the prison setting. As Figure 6.4 shows, staff indicated eleven factors of which "inmate behavior" and "confrontation with inmates" ranked highest. Once again, "management techniques" was found to be one of the least significant variables in the list, a viewpoint that is greatly in contrast with most administrators' ideology.

Figure 6.3.

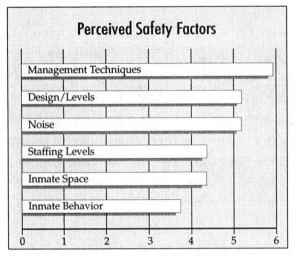

(1=greatest importance, 6=least importance)

Source: *Corrections Today,* 1997

Figure 6.4

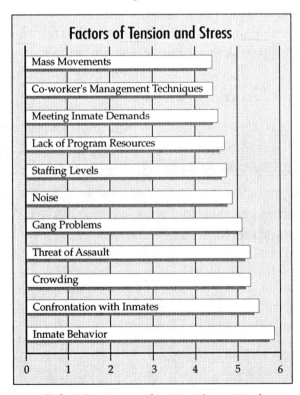

(1=least importance, 6=greatest importance)

Source: *Corrections Today,* 1997

Rostad and Witke (1997) also surveyed prison staff to ascertain what changes they believed were necessary to address the issues of assault, control, and safety. As shown in Figure 6.5, "more staff training" ranked highest among the offered suggestions with "increased programming and/or work assignment" following in second place. Once again, the opinions of those on staff who perhaps have the greatest contact with the prison culture (besides the prisoners themselves) seemed to have a somewhat different understanding of what responses would be most effective in dealing with institutional security issues.

Figure 6.5

Correctional Staffs' Proposed Changes to Increase Prison Safety

Stricter Rules
Reduced Noise Levels
Reduced Blind Spots
Increased Programming
More Staff Training

0 1 2 3 4 5 6 7 8

(1=least importance, 8=greatest importance)

Source: *Corrections Today,* **1997**

Expert Views of Proper Correctional Management

Despite the lack of importance some attach to management issues, in their book, Bert Useem and Peter Kimball (1991) discuss many ideas about how proper correctional management can lessen the probability of a riot occurring in a prison. They see good administration as the key to safe prison management. This "good administration" is operationalized as proper programming, opportunities for inmate work and activities, and concerns about crowding and the amenities of life in general. They hold that it is the disorganization of the state (in other words, disorganization in correctional management, problems in prison administration, and so forth) not the organization of inmates that is crucial in running any correctional facility. Quality of leadership was reported as one area that could not be overestimated in managing prisons; people will follow a leader who has consistent policies.

Useem and Kimball (1991) and the American Correctional Association (1996) empha-size that communication is important in a prison setting. Prison administrators who communicate with their entire organization and regularly deal with surfacing problems are likely to avoid prison disturbances through early detection and diffusion practices. Useem and Kimball reported that positive motivation was a key strategy. The effective warden will develop programs that promote positive attitudes regarding the institu-tion, leaving the few disgruntled members without a following. They also discuss the problems with antiquated prisons. These very often are institutions, which are packed with populations of violent individuals but lack any productive activities or programs for them. These institutions become void of any hope (among both correctional staff and inmates) and pose serious threats to institutional safety and tranquility.

Dr. Ellis MacDougall's Ideas

Dr. Ellis MacDougall (Braswell, Dillingham, and Montgomery, 1985) reported that a major contributor to institutional violence is insufficient prison space. He also com-mented on another explosive factor, the inmate personality. He felt that most riots took place in maximum-security institutions. MacDougall stated that most of the time, bore-dom and the absence of meaningful employment, educational, and vocational opportu-nities contributed to prison violence and riots. Change was also an important factor discussed by Ellis MacDougall and Reid Montgomery (1986), one which they felt must be understood by prison administrators. Casual and hasty rule changes may cause rip-ples of discontent that soon will increase in magnitude.

Knowledge of Security-threat Groups

A study conducted by the American Correctional Association (1993) suggested that security-threat groups were responsible for approximately 20 percent of the violence toward prison staff and 40 percent of the violence directed toward prisoners. The American Correctional Association's advisory board also offered a definition of what constituted a security-threat group (STG):

> Two or more inmates, acting together, who pose a threat to the security or safety of staff/inmates and/or are disruptive to programs and/or to the orderly management of the facility/system.

A study conducted in 1991 by G. W. Knox and E. D. Tromhanauser estimated that as many as 100,000 inmates belonged to a prison gang. A subsequent study (American Correctional Association, 1993) revealed less than half that number. Regardless of the exact number of inmates involved in prison gangs or other security-threat groups, some prison administrators are reluctant to acknowledge the growing problem that these groups present. This "denial" has resulted in a very small number of gang-tracking systems (record-keeping and monitoring) across the country.

Robert Levinson (1994), in an American Correctional Association study, determined the prevalence of prison gangs or security-threat groups in the fifty-two prison systems across the United States. The following is a listing of the top ten-most reported groups:

Figure 6.6 Prison Gangs Across the United States

Group Name	Number of Systems Reporting Group	Percentage of Institutions in which Gangs Listed are Present
Aryan Brotherhood	29	57
Crips	29	57
Skinheads	26	51
Bloods	26	51
White Supremacy Group	24	47
Ku Klux Klan	20	39
Nation of Islam	19	37
Black Disciples	18	35
Latin Kings	18	35
Hells Angels	17	33

Source: Levinson, Prison Gangs: A National Assessment

Several academic studies suggest that modern American correctional facilities provide fertile environments for the growth of gangs. In 1985, McConville stated that gangs have the capability to expand or sustain themselves in a prison environment if the following circumstances are prevalent:

- Inmates are permitted somewhat free mobility in the cell blocks and other parts of the institution
- Staff oversight was remote, rather than direct
- Inadequate protection of the general population by prison staff
- Inability to control contraband (smuggling, sales, trade, and so forth)
- Free or unfettered communication with the outside world

Some of the recent rise in state prison populations is the result of the increased time inmates are serving. Yet, data on prison admissions and releases collected annually in the National Corrections Reporting Program (NCRP) (Bureau of Justice Statistics, 1997b) reveal that growth in state prison populations has not been the result of longer sentences imposed, but rather a larger percentage of the sentences imposed being served. Between 1985 and 1995, the average (mean) sentence of prisoners declined from seventy-eight months to sixty-six months. The median length of imposed sentences for prisoners admitted from court remained constant at forty-eight months. Moreover, despite the increasing use of mandatory minimums and sentencing enhancements during the period, the percentage of inmates who received a maximum sentence of ten years or longer also declined (from 19.7 percent in 1985 to 17.1 percent in 1995).

Walking Around and Other Management Strategies

One effective management tool is correctional managers simply walking around their institutions. Often, this allows the managers to diagnose institutional problems and/or identify indicators in their environment that may be warning signs of pending violence or disruption. Such a strategy also provides inmates and staff with a direct grievance mechanism between the inmates and the prison administration.

Grievance Process

A grievance mechanism is a method, according to the National Institute of Corrections, for resolving inmate complaints. A grievance usually involves a complaint about the substance or application of a written or unwritten policy or regulation. Normally, the grievance is filed in a written complaint. Then, a hearing is held where the grievance is resolved. At this type of hearing, all parties are in attendance to determine whether policy is being complied with both by the correctional staff and the inmate. At this point, remedies are sought to correct any errors that may be occurring.

Ombudsperson

Another strategy for correctional departments is the use of an ombudsperson. Such a person performs in a capacity similar to an inspector general in the military. This person has the power to ameliorate problem situations and render satisfactory responses to legitimate problems.

Inmate Councils

Through interaction with these inmate-elected bodies, inmates are able to express their concerns. Inmate representatives are individuals who have been elected to their positions by fellow inmates. Arrangements typically are made for inmate representatives to discuss with other inmates their major concerns and anxieties. Inmates who have suggestions, problems, complaints, or grievances are able to communicate them to their inmate representative, who, in turn, relays the information to the inmate council. Concerns are related to the warden for resolution.

Inmate Inventories

These are written instruments which wardens can use to detect riot-prone conditions. The inmate inventory uses a Likert scale of measurement. For example, one item might be a chance to see the warden. The inmate is provided two words at the opposite ends of the scale. One word is the word "easy" and the other word is "difficult." Five spaces numbered one to five are provided for the inmate to mark his or her feelings on this particular item. Inmate inventories can be administered by wardens to a random sample at their institution each month. If, for example, 90 percent of the inmates marked dissatisfied with the medical treatment, then the warden would have a definite need to investigate and correct the perceived problem area.

Prison Tactical Teams

These teams are essential for modern correctional systems (*Corrections Compendium*, April, 1996). These teams can be used for a show of force to deter prison violence and as an effective tool in containing, controlling, and resolving violent incidents according to experts. These emergency response teams are referred to by many names: Special Weapons and Tactics (SWAT), Special Emergency Response Team (SERT), Correctional Emergency Response Team (CERT), Tactical Response Team (TRT), Special Reaction Team (SRT), and Special Operations Response Team (SORT).

Art Programs

Many feel that art programs pay for themselves in reduced cost for correctional staff and for vandalism. Furthermore, arts are a time-management tool for prison administration (Farrer, 1995; Gutierrez-McDermid, 1995). They give offenders a positive way to deal with their leisure time. Oklahoma, for example, has one of the largest and most effective prison arts programs. Classes are held at fifteen institutions and involve over 3,000 inmates. Classes include dance, theater, music, photography, and sculpture (Crews, Montgomery, and Garris, 1996).

Post-occupancy Evaluations (POEs)

These evaluations collect data on facility design and policy in an organized, systematic, and reliable manner and present the findings clearly. For example, inmates, line staff, maintenance staff, and management provide input. Systematic observations, interviews, and surveys are the main tools used to evaluate a facility. The POEs help prison administrators correct current problems as well as influence design improvements for new institutions.

Classification of Inmates

The AIMS (Adult Internal Management System) approach, for example, classifies inmates objectively into one of three groups (Crews, et al., 1996): *alphas* (who are the most aggressive and may be leaders); *betas* (who are dependent, often ask for help, and usually are passive but may explode, if provoked); and *gammas* (who are neither aggressive nor dependent, are more cooperative, have less criminal history, and avoid trouble). A life history checklist and a correctional adjustment checklist help prison authorities determine in which of the three categories to place each inmate. Ideally, each group would be housed separately. Furthermore, if unit management is used, the staff of each unit can act more in line with the type of inmates assigned to the unit. Unit management combines line correctional officers and case workers into one unit. This approach breaks the barrier between uniformed and nonuniformed staff in that the characteristics of an institution's correctional staff can be paired with the characteristics of the inmates in a particular housing area.

Extensive Training

Correctional personnel should receive training in how to recognize signs of tension in their prisons. One such course, "Containment of Prison Violence" was created by the National Institute of Corrections (1982). There are many signs of impending problems that may erupt into riots and disturbances. The National Institute of Corrections categorizes them, as shown in Figure 6.7:

Figure 6.7. Signs of Problems that May Erupt into Riots or Disturbances

1. Restlessness among inmates
2. Quiet or subdued actions of inmate groups
3. Avoidance of visual and/or verbal contact with staff
4. Increase in commissary purchases
5. Increase in the number of requests for assignment changes
6. Unusual inmate gatherings
7. Increase in the number of incident reports
8. Appearance of inflammatory written material
9. Absence of inmates at popular functions
10. Increase in the number of complaints
11. Disturbances at other institutions
12. Assault on an individual of another race or group

Alternatives to Violence Project (AVP)

This project currently is being used with inmates at New York State's Elmira
Correctional Facility (Crews, et al., 1996). This twenty-two-hour workshop teaches
inmates how to deal with violence that exists in their facility. Inmates take part in activities designed to break down barriers, increase relaxation and fun, build community
spirit, examine self-violence, explore how violence escalates, and teach intervention
methods. Trainers show inmates that the principles of nonviolence can work in their
daily lives. For example, in prison society, if one inmate takes another inmate's sneak-
ers, the victim inmate usually responds by assaulting the inmate who took his shoes.
The Alternatives to Violence Project teaches inmates that there are alternatives to
assaulting fellow inmates in these incidents.

Alternatives to Incarceration

Many feel that strategies must be employed prior to many individuals ever entering an
institution and assist in reducing the booming prison population. Alternatives might
include greater use of probation/parole, day reporting centers, work release centers,
boot camps, halfway houses, electronic monitoring, and intensive supervision (Crews,
et al., 1996).

Current Trends

There are many contemporary movements, ideologies, and trends which are beginning to play a large role in the control and maintenance of America's correctional facilities. The following list is a brief overview of the major strategies, issues, and concerns influencing current correctional practices:

- Tighter budgets demand creativity in prison design and management techniques

- Cost-effective construction (building one large institution in lieu of many smaller institutions)

- Enhanced involvement of elected officials in prison management

- Increasingly conservative public attitudes towards offenders

- Conservative management

- Harsher sentencing practices (longer, determinate sentencing)

- Trend of abolishing parole

- Drastic increase in violent juvenile offenders (baby boom echo)

- Privatization and contracting with the private sector

- New food service technologies (revamping of outdated or inadequate food service)

- New technology allowing inmates to receive visitors without leaving cells (remote visitation)

- Increased use of "Emergency Response" technologies (coordination of emergency units)

The Importance of Inmate Families

A key element in maintaining a safe prison environment, which often is overlooked, is the motivation of the inmate to control his or her behavior. An extremely important factor in inmates' motivation is their relationship with their families. Accompanying the population explosion within the modern prison system are the forgotten family members who also experience high levels of trauma and loss. There are approximately 1.5 million children in the United States who have a parent in jail or prison (Johnston, 1995; Blinn, 1997). These children often inherit many of their incarcerated parents' problems (such as the inability to communicate effectively, difficulty maintaining relationships, and limited coping skills). The obstacle of the prison sentence in the relationships between the inmate and his or her family only serves to foster an atmosphere of estrangement.

Families must learn to deal with the demoralization caused by the shame and stigma of a family member in prison and establish new relationships with a person who now is "living while dead" (Schwartz and Weintraub, 1974). The atmosphere often is strained and tense when families visit an incarcerated relative. Inmates are oftentimes uncomfortable or silent during visits with their families (Adalist-Estrin, 1995). Yet, staying in touch is important. As a management tool, administrators should encourage such visits. Inmates who get out of control can lose the privilege of having visitors, something very valuable to them.

According to George Roof, the Assistant Director of Security, South Carolina Department of Corrections, quality of life in a prison setting often can be gauged subjectively by examining the atmosphere for things such as:

- Tension
- Feelings of hostility between the inmates, or between the inmates and the correctional officers
- The cleanliness of the prison
- The level to which the staff feel safe (or threatened)
- Whether the inmates feel the institution is a good place in which to serve time

Since the inception of the first "visitation" programs in the early 1700s, prison officials have been witnesses to the impact that family contact has on prison inmates. Several contemporary studies have found positive relationships between the maintenance of strong family ties during imprisonment and post-release success (Ohlin, 1951; Adams and Fischer, 1976; Holt and Miller, 1972). In 1988, Hairston stated that the social network that families provide protects a person from a variety of stressful stimuli typically experienced in a prison setting (such as fear of abandonment, loss of self-worth, and other issues).

Perhaps the most important effect that a family can have on incarcerated relatives is to provide them with the necessary motivation to better themselves in a fashion that will serve them best in the future (by participating in educational, substance-abuse, or religious programs, or developing job and communication skills). This promoted level of "hope" is a key element in maintaining a safe prison environment. The motivated inmate is less likely to participate in a riot. An inmate with the perception of having nothing to loose can prove to be an institutional danger.

The American Correctional Association standards for Adult Correctional Institutions (1990b and 1998) recognize the important role that family plays in the inmate's rehabilitation process and has several standards to facilitate these relationships. Following are some examples of standards intended to help guide and foster family ties while maintaining a safe prison environment.

Visitation Length (3-4440): Written policy, procedure, and practice provide that the number of visitors an inmate may receive and the length of visits may be limited only by the institution's schedule, space, and personnel constraints, or when there are substantial reasons to justify such limitations.

Visiting (3-4441): Written policy, procedure, and practice provide that inmate visiting facilities permit informal communication, including opportunity for physical contact. Devices that preclude physical contact are not used except in instances of substantiated security risk.

Visiting Information (3-4441-1): Written policy, procedure, and practice provide that written information regarding procedures governing visitation be made available to the inmate within 24 hours after arrival at the facility. At a minimum, the information will include, but not be limited to, the following: a) facility address/phone number, directions to facility and information about local transportation, b) days and hours of visitation, c) approved dress code and identification requirements for visitors, d) items authorized in visitation room, e) special rules for children, f) authorized items that visitors may bring to give to offender (for example, funds, pictures, etc.), and g) special visits (for example, family emergencies).

Current Correctional Practices to Deal with the Threat of Prison Violence

General Emergency Preparedness

At times, the daily operations of running a modern American correctional institution seem almost impossible. The reality of crowding, idleness, boredom, apathy, lack of resources, and other management problems can foster an environment of frustration and uneasiness in an inmate population. Outside noninstitutional events often can spark adverse inmate reactions inside an institution, causing unexpected violent incidents to occur. Correctional institutions must remain at a level of emergency preparedness, and staff must be ready to react immediately and adequately in the event that a situation arises (Henderson, Rauch, and Phillips, 1997). Incidents can arise instantly, but emergency preparedness and emergency plans cannot.

There is debate as to the best response in an emergency situation. Some believe that an immediate aggressive response is the most effective response, while others believe that many situations require a more measured approach. Often, response decisions are based on a correctional manager's past experience and personal belief system.

Although the debate goes on, there generally are actions which are agreed upon that must occur in any emergency situation.

The safety of the public must be of paramount concern; therefore, a strong perimeter must be established and maintained. The crisis itself must be contained to the minimum area possible within the institution, and all staff must be accounted for and safe. The appropriate officials and necessary staff must be notified, and all local and agency-wide resources must be gathered. Also as a backdrop to all of the emergency activities is preserving whatever evidence is possible for future prosecution of those involved (Henderson, Rauch, and Phillips, 1998, p. 180).

There also must be careful consideration about the various areas of an institution that must be contained during any prison crisis. Files and areas that may hold official records or inmate files must be protected, as well as those areas which contain tools and weapons. Often, the drugs in medical areas are targeted, and commissaries are ransacked. The kitchen is another area that must be secured as soon as possible in that it is a source for weapons and food.

Hostage Plans

A hostage is any person (an employee, visitor, or inmate) who is held against his or her will by another person for purposes of escape or monetary gain, or in any other manner that places that hostage in danger of bodily injury or death. No person, regardless of rank or status, has any authority while being held hostage. Hostage-taking is one of the most dangerous events that a correctional manger will face and one that occurs as either a spur-of-the-moment action or a premeditated act. Correctional managers must be cognizant of staff who have a higher potential of being taken hostage—employees alone in isolated areas, or staff in offices without proper windows (Henderson, Rauch, and Phillips, 1997; see also McMains and Mullens, 1996).

In the event of a hostage-taking incident, there also are generally agreed-upon actions that must be taken by correctional officials as soon as possible. The perimeter should be altered and reinforced, and a general lockdown should be considered. Any available trained hostage negotiators should be summoned and tactical personnel should obtain equipment and prepare for action. As with any emergency situation, all appropriate administration and staff must be notified (*Corrections Compendium*, July, 1995).

As the situation develops, the warden must consider each move very carefully and evaluate all possible approaches to the situation. The warden can contain the situation and demand surrender or choose to negotiate surrender and the release of all hostages. Using chemical agents to force surrender and employing snipers or sharpshooters to disable the hostage taker(s), or the deploying of tactical staff for an actual assault are always options (Freeman, 1996).

One of the most pressing decisions to be made when a disturbance occurs is whether to use force or negotiate. History has demonstrated that, while an immediate aggressive response is effective, if it falls short of its intended result, it is almost impossible to then move to negotiation.

Therefore, the decision for an initial course of action often will dictate what choices are to be made as the event continues. If negotiation is the response that is chosen, the first objective is to convince a hostage taker to safely release the hostages and to surrender. To build relationships with the hostage taker, negotiations should be conducted author- itatively, but at the same time, the negotiator must let the hostage taker know that nego- tiators have no final authority. Everything discussed in negotiations must be approved by someone higher in the organization. The hostage taker's family or friends should not be brought to the scene in that this may provoke a violent outburst, but a mental health professional should be standing by for consultation, if an extended situation develops. A bullhorn or public address system should not be used for negotiations unless there is no other alternative, because the impersonal nature of these methods may interfere with the development of trust and rapport in the negotiation process.

If negotiations cannot be conducted safely face-to-face, which is often the case, then the phone system should be used. Negotiation over the phone allows a personal, private conversation and provides the negotiator with a maximum amount of protection and safety. It also enables the isolation and simplification of the negotiation process. Face-to- face negotiations allow more accurate assessment of the mental state of the hostage taker, but should be undertaken only after rapport has been established through some other mode of communication. They should be carried out only from a safe position; often some form of barricade is needed to assure that the negotiator is not harmed or taken captive (National Institute of Corrections, 1982).

A key principle of hostage negotiations is the likelihood that hostages will be released unharmed as time passes. This is because the basic needs for normal intake patterns of food and water, and regular sleep, increase as time passes. The anxiety and tension of the initial situation tend to abate over time; most persons begin to think more rationally and less emotionally after the early stage of a crisis passes (Henderson, Rauch, and Phillips, 1997, p. 224).

Security Audits

If the lessons of past riots have taught anything, they have taught that correctional officials cannot wait until security systems break down to decide to fix them. If officials wait until there is a problem, this practice allows inmates to find the flaws in a security system first, while correctional workers assume all is well and find themselves in a false sense of security. In almost every reported correctional disturbance in American history, poor security practices often preceded or at least aggravated the incident (Czerniak and Upchurch, 1996).

There are many examples of where poor security practices have led to escapes or prison disturbances. They may include failure by officers to check identification cards and to properly perform strip searches. Sleeping in tower or perimeter posts, poor tool and key control, and the failure to make security checks, are just a few of those examples (Czerniak and Upchurch, 1996).

A solution to this problem is to maintain an active program of security audits. The primary purpose of conducting a security audit is to identify weaknesses or deficiencies in a security operation so that corrective actions can be taken to strengthen it. Auditing should determine whether any security breaches are occurring. First, institution procedures must comply with agency policy and be sufficient to prevent security problems; if there are any actual security deficiencies, the audit process should identify the specific actions needed to correct them. Second, actual practices should be in accord with written procedures, and staff should be capable of appropriately responding to hypothetical situations posed by the auditors (Silberman, 1995).

Security Equipment

In any type of emergency-preparedness effort, the checking of security equipment cannot be overlooked. The following is a list of the basic security-related equipment items that an institution should have and that should be checked on an ongoing basis:

- Emergency generator
- X-ray or other scanning equipment
- Walk-through metal detectors
- Perimeter detection system
- Fence wire
- Lighting
- Tower intercoms
- Standardized key storage cabinets
- Key machine

- Audio-dialer
- Two-way radio systems
- Closed-circuit television
- Public address systems
- Automated/remotely actuated gates, grilles, doors
- Ordnance (rifles, shotguns, handguns, gas projectiles, and so forth)
- Personal body alarms and receivers
- Patrol vehicles and transport vehicles (Henderson, Rauch, and Phillips, 1997).

Use of Force

Remember, when force is absolutely necessary, staff must use only the minimum amount necessary to prevent escapes and to protect the public. Force can be used to control an inmate to ensure the safety of staff, inmates, and others in the institution. It also can be used to prevent serious property damage and to ensure institution security and safety (Skovron, 1988).

Training is critical in dealing with the use of force. Correctional staff must be aware of the departmental policy on the use of force, especially deadly force. They need to know when to use force and how much to use. The best way to ensure this is to conduct initial and annual refresher training for all staff. The training should include a detailed presentation on the departmental philosophy related to the use of force and its relationship to successful inmate management (Henderson, Rauch, and Phillips, 1997).

Tactical Operations and Emergency Response Teams

The current wave of federal and state legislation has promised to keep prisons filled as quickly as they can be constructed. With a prison population that has passed one million inmates, it is no wonder why prisons have and will continue to explode in violent incidents. With the number of disturbances and riots, inmate-on-inmate and inmate-on-staff assaults continue to increase, but correctional institutions must be prepared to respond.

Historically (*Corrections Compendium*, July, 1995), American prisons have created emergency response teams by recruiting the largest and most aggressive correctional officers that could be found. This brought about the portrayal of these emergency response teams as being "goon squads" that would come into any situation and "bust heads." The results of such a practice became very clear in the Attica prison riot in 1971. This riot left $2 million dollars in property damage and forty-three dead. The state police officers retaking the prison killed twenty-nine prisoners and eleven

Sniper rifle. (*Source:* South Carolina Department of Corrections)

prison-employee hostages. This riot resulted in numerous lawsuits challenging prison conditions and the lethal response by prison officials. From events such as this, American prison officials began to see the need for on-call highly trained strike teams to respond to emergency situations.

Thus, correctional facilities around the country sought experts in law enforcement to assist in the development of emergency response teams (*Corrections Compendium*, July, 1995). Many departments modeled their response teams after Police SWAT Teams and other military commando units such as the Army Green Beret Special Forces, and the Navy Seal teams. These teams were composed of members who were trained to be snipers, to rescue hostages, and to storm prisons.

Tactical teams should be equipped suitably for personal protection, as well as to perform the assigned task. Typical issue items include: gas masks, protective helmet and face guards, jump suits, batons and protective shields, bullet-proof vests, and steel and plastic handcuffs. Firearms, chemical agents, and other ordnance, including remote grenades, stun rounds, sting balls, and flash rounds often are employed by these teams (*Corrections Compendium*, July, 1995).

Staff from other agencies may need to be contacted to supplement the institutional security force. State highway patrol, municipal police departments, and county sheriff's departments need to be notified, as do local fire departments, local ambulance services, and even possibly civil defense. The National Guard is also an option that may need to be considered (Freeman, 1996).

Proper intelligence gathering often is crucial to the effectiveness of any emergency response team. The location and nature of the disturbance, and the extent of damage, as well as the location of any barricades, blocked grilles or doors, or other hindrances to tactical operations is absolutely necessary for any decision making on how and when an emergency team is to be used. The number of hostages held and the number of persons needing aid is also very crucial. Of course, the approximate number of inmates involved and the types of weapons and equipment being used by inmates must be as accurate as possible (*Corrections Compendium*, July, 1995).

There are also various suggestions about the proper supervision that must occur as soon as a disturbance is under control. Appropriate follow-up steps must be followed. Proper supervision must be maintained on site after a disturbance to ensure that the command staff act properly in their subduing, restraining, searching, and moving of inmates to secure housing. Care must be taken to prevent any retaliatory action against inmates by correctional staff. Generally, there are agreed upon follow-up steps that should be taken during any postincident action. All leaders and agitators must be segregated and appropriate care taken of all nonparticipants. Correctional officials must account for all inmates and staff members. As with any prison disturbance, a thorough investigation into the cause and course of a disturbance must be conducted. Interviews of all those involved in the disturbance must be conducted and their statements must be obtained for subsequent prosecutions. Immediately, repairs to institutional physical security features should be made. However, security staff should be sure to photograph all damage before making the repairs (Henderson, Rauch, and Phillips, 1997).

Futuristic Approaches to Prison Management and Control

The following is an examination of various proposed futuristic approaches to prison management and inmate control. Many of these ideas are actually in use today in many correctional institutions and used by American law enforcement. Several scenarios are very futuristic and may not be seen for many decades from now, if ever. The purpose of this section is to offer the reader food for thought about what measures the United States and the world now are taking and may have to take in the near future to deal with the growing numbers of inmates. While some of these options may never be realized, they are included to expand the thinking of those in corrections so that by offering some far out solutions, one can explore a wide range of options.

Alcatraz of the Rockies

One of the most advanced maximum-security prison systems in the world is in Florence, Colorado. Its nickname is the "Alcatraz of the Rockies." This institution is a prototype of the kinds of institutions that may be seen across the United States in the near future.

This institution has 1,400 electronically controlled gates, 168 video cameras, and can house 484 inmates. Dangerous inmates are kept in their cells twenty-three hours a day. The worst inmates are allowed out of their cells only if they have on leg irons and hand-cuffs and are escorted by several guards.

This prison has some unique features:

> . . . inside the cells, all furniture is immobile: a cement stool, a cement desk, a cement bed, a cement stand that holds a 12 inch black and white TV. There is no soap dish, knob, toilet seat or toilet handle—all potential weapons have been made unavailable. Inmates use powdered soap; soap bars can be turned into knives (Crews, Montgomery, Garris, 1996).

The visiting room has a glass window that can withstand two hours of pounding with a hammer. Visitors speak by phones to inmates and sit on lightweight, nonflammable plastic chairs. The cement walls are 5,000 pound quality. Additionally, steel bars criss-cross the inside every eight inches. Education courses and religious services are regularly broadcast on television. Showers and sinks are electronically timed to prevent flooding.

Cells are strategically angled so inmates cannot see other cells or the Rocky Mountains from their small windows. Also, this prevents communication between prisoners and denies inmates a sense of where they are if they try to escape. All cell doors open electronically. When the door opens, the inmate walks alone to the recreation area, a cement room containing a chin-up bar. When he is done, he will walk back, the door opening and closing behind him. The prison has four emergency generators, each capable of lighting a town of 800 houses.

Six guard towers are at different heights to thwart air attack and allow for clear views of the roof. Metal flaps cover the contours of keys of correctional officers so that prisoners cannot memorize the ridges and make their own. To get out, inmates must pass through as many as seven three-inch-thick steel doors, each one opening only after the other has closed. If one guard station is seized, all controls are switched to the next station. If the whole prison is seized, it can be controlled from outside. The worst inmates get no television and just one fifteen-minute phone call every three months.

Technology-based Futuristic Approaches

Video Visitation

In another scenario, used at the "Alcatraz of the Rockies," traditional visitation within a penal institution is replaced by communication between the inmate and another actor via video conference. This method proves itself worthy in many respects. It eliminates the amount of contraband that is typically smuggled in during face-to-face visitations, and provides a greater sense of security for visitor, inmate, and correctional staff involved. Video visitation also allows prisoners to communicate with individuals they otherwise may not have had access to for long periods of time (such as relatives living great distances, busy lawyers, and so forth).

The benefits that such technology brings is not just limited to the concept of visitation but rather, it also may play a large role in courtroom appearances and investigation. This new ability to communicate via phone or satellite also would allow the building of prisons in more remote areas without raising the cost of transportation or reducing the number of visitors who feasibly can travel such a distance (Crews, Montgomery, and Garris, 1996). Additionally, video now is being used to replace, in certain cases, court appearances and for telemedicine. The use of video is expected to increase.

Global Positioning System (GPS)

In the future, technology now used for other purposes may be brought to bear on riot prevention and the limiting or quashing of riots in correctional facilities. Such ideas may seem futuristic, but they are presented to stimulate thought on this topic. Out of dreams, reality may be fashioned.

Remote-sensing satellites will enable prison officials to keep track of ex-offenders once they leave prison. They also may be the ultimate weapon in preventing prison riots, which may have a true goal of mass escape. Employing this concept, every prison can be watched night and day from space satellites.

Faceprints to Produce Positive Identification

Inmates who are classified as dangerous, generally, do not move freely inside an institution. "Faceprints" would allow correctional staff to identify inmates immediately and determine if an inmate is in the proper location. This system using infrared sensors can recognize an individual's facial thermogram. A person's unique pattern is created by the heat-emitting veins and arteries on the face which the computer stores in its memory.

The system consists of a camera and a computer database of facial thermograms. For identification, an individual stands in front of the camera and types a personal identification number into the computer. Using the identification number, the computer calls up a stored image and matches it with the live image of the person standing before the camera. The technology is so advanced that persons who have had plastic surgery will not confuse the system (Crews, Montgomery, and Garris, 1996).

Electroshock Monitoring

With electroshock monitoring, all inmates would wear a receiver around their ankle. A radio "fence" would be built around the correctional institution. Inmates who try to cross this boundary would receive an electrical shock strong enough to knock them down. Some courts across the United States use court monitoring systems where inmates wearing belts receive a shock if they become disruptive in the courtroom.

Watch Patrol

Expanding on telemetry systems now in use, inmates who have followed the rules and not participated in violence inside the correctional institution, likely will qualify for a furlough. To keep an inmate under surveillance while on furlough, they will be required to wear a "watch patrol" watch. A tamper check is made every second on the watch so that the inmate cannot alter it. Furthermore, the watch patrol takes advantage of the caller identification infrastructure provided by the telecommunications industry to positively establish an offender's location rather than relying on expensive and sometimes unreliable radio equipment.

Bar Codes

One way to watch inmates is through the use of bar codes. These codes would be scanned and a corresponding computer would access the inmate's information file. A correctional officer using a scanner can check whether an inmate should have a razor or not. If inmates are on suicide watch, they would not be allowed to have a razor. Using a scanner, a correctional officer could check if an inmate should be in certain locations. Also, the correctional officer could check on inmate property to prevent theft by other inmates.

Sticky Foam

One way to control inmates who become violent would be for the correctional officer to spray them with a sticky foam. This technology currently is being tested at various police departments and by the U.S. Marine Corps. Sticky foam stops a suspect because everything it touches becomes stuck to it, immobilizing the subject's legs and arms like contact cement. Sticky foam might help to capture rioters if exits were blocked with large bags filled with the substance through which a rioter would have to pass to escape riot squads. If rioters broke the bag, they would be engulfed in the sticky foam (Crews, Montgomery, and Garris, 1996).

Smart Guns

Technology could enable only correctional officers with the ability to fire weapons to do so during a riot. Computerized sensors could ensure that the person who fires the weapon is the person who is authorized to use it.

Ultrasound

Ultrasound might be a technique useful to end prison riots in a matter of seconds. Sound devices could be installed in correctional facilities. These devices would produce high-intensity sound waves. Rioting inmates would be knocked unconscious for several minutes when the sound waves hit their eardrums. Correctional officers, on the other hand, would wear special helmets to protect their eardrums (Crews, Montgomery, and Garris, 1996).

Robots

Today, robots already perform dangerous or repetitive tasks in the industrial workforce. Applied to corrections, robots may be used to guard prisons, performing many of the monotonous yet dangerous tasks that human correctional officers must handle each day. Robots already are being developed for security use. For example, Denning Mobile Robotics Company produces a robot named the "Denny." This robot is four feet tall, weighs 400 pounds, and costs $30,000. It can track unauthorized intruders with infrared and ultrasonic sensors and an ammonia "sniffer" that will detect odor given off by humans. Some of these robots also are equipped with television cameras.

The features developed for the Denny would be valuable in correctional disturbances or riots. For instance, robots equipped with cameras could photograph a prison riot in progress, enabling the prison administration to detect the cause and primary instigators of the riot. In addition, videotaping a riot will provide evidence for any later prosecution or lawsuits.

Robots could be implanted with a device to enable them to know the correct response in different types of rioting situations. Proper computer programs would ensure that all the robots are responding in a coordinated manner.

Suspended Animation

Suspended animation (cryogenics) might be a useful technique for highly violent inmates. However, as of now, no known cryogenic defrosting system is operational. So, the following technique may be far into the future. The Quay classification system identifies highly aggressive inmates as "alphas." A futuristic prison system might place "alphas" in suspended animation for their period of confinement. It is better to have a sleeping lion than a roaring one.

Telepathic Skills

A warning of coming riots could be achieved by developing the telepathic skills of correctional staff. Note that today, many correctional officers "sense" a change of behavior that is indicative of a riot about to occur. Staff with this ability could "read the minds of riot-plotting inmates."

Undersea Prisons and Space Prisons

Right now it sounds far out, but as property for the siting of prisons becomes more valuable, innovative systems may consider undersea prisons. Huge prisons built on the floor of the ocean would present little opportunity for prisoners to escape. Inmates in these correctional facilities could be used to harvest sea vegetation and drill for oil. Even greater security could be achieved by building space prisons. Few inmates would want to take part in a riot that possibly could damage their supply of oxygen.

Rehabilitation and Treatment-based Futuristic Approaches

Pet Therapy

Another therapy type of program which is not very futuristic in nature is pet therapy. Prison experts have found that aggressive inmates relax when they take part in pet therapy programs. Taking care of the animals teaches them to behave gently while in a harsh environment. Such therapeutic techniques will reduce an individual's predisposition to violence and work to rehabilitate an inmate, preparing the inmate for the eventual return to society (Crews, Montgomery, and Garris, 1996).

Space, Color, and Lighting

Correctional institutions in the future should emphasize improved use of space, color, and lighting. The double-bunked, crowded cells evident in correctional institutions could be modified greatly, allowing each inmate more humane living conditions. Correctional institutions in the future should implement structural changes such as the more frequent use of plexiglass in place of bricks and bars, and a greater use of sky-lights. As a result, inmates' perceptions of their confinement may be more positive; they will feel less like caged animals and more like human beings. When they feel they are treated better, they may react in a less hostile manner. Prisons in the future also should emphasize constructive use of color. Recent studies indicate the calming effects of soft pastel colors on jail inmates (Crews, Montgomery, and Garris, 1996). In the correctional setting, color could serve as a control mechanism, calming the inmates and hence preventing disruptive behavior.

Television Programming for Inmates

One way to change violent behavior of some inmates is through the use of television programming. As discussed in the Introduction of this book, there is a strong link between the types of television programs watched and human behavior. For example, these inmates could be required to watch television programs on topics such as: drug and alcohol treatment, education, vocational training, employment readiness, parenting skills, anger management, and prevention of domestic violence. Remote learning is already in place in many locations.

Subliminal Messages

Correctional institutions might use subliminal messages to influence inmate behavior. Subliminal anti-riot messages might include the following: "Do the right thing," "Obey the prison rules," "Don't take part in a riot," and "Do your own time; don't let others influence you the wrong way." These subliminal messages could be mixed with background music twenty-four hours a day in jails and prisons. Courts even might sentence offenders to have subliminal anti-riot microplayers implanted.

Brain Peptides and Chemicals

Brain peptides and chemicals might be used by medically trained correctional personnel to control an inmate's emotional behavior. It is known, for example, that high levels of serotonin can control aggression. With the aid of a peptide implant, this chemical could be released automatically, lowering a person's level of aggression. Through the implanting of brain chemicals, undesired behavior could be controlled. Implementation of ideas such as this will serve as fertile grounds for court litigation in the near future.

Correctional Managers of Today Preparing for Tomorrow

It is a common belief that because something is done in a particular fashion that it, indeed, is the "best" way. However, as the world of corrections changes, correctional administrators and staff also must change to meet the day's new challenges. Administrators who have reached a maturing plateau in their careers often find that the skills they have assimilated into their arsenals throughout their years are no longer as effective. If this is the case, then correctional managers of the modern era constantly must be exposed to the latest in technology and philosophy to maintain a dominant hand in their changing world.

Conclusion

"Communication," according to Dr. Vernon Fox (1997), describes the best course prison personnel can take to prevent prison riots. Fox held that the administration and staff who systematically communicated with inmates provided an outlet through which inmates were able to express their concerns without resorting to violence.

The enduring theme of inmate frustration can be understood best by examining the literary works of famous inmate authors throughout history. George Jackson (the death of this inmate leader, admired by inmates around the country in the late 1960s, in a California prison added to the tension in Attica prior to its famous riot in 1971) once wrote, "I'll never again relax. I'll never make peace with this world as long as the enemies of self-determination have the running of things" (Jackson, 1970, p. 235). This quote is symbolic of the lack of control and self-determination that inmates feel in America's prisons. Increasing tension within any prison setting can build up and potentially materialize in the form of a riot. Perhaps a greater understanding of the dynamics of a riot and better communication between actors could have prevented the New Mexico Penitentiary riot of 1980. An inmate, weeks prior to the riot had stated,

" . . . the prison's going to blow." This statement was publicly made, yet no actions were taken to change or to deter the explosive riot that soon followed (Morris, 1993, p.19).

The New York Special Commission on Attica (1972) illustrated the importance of the inmate/correctional officer relationship, enhanced by effective communication:

> The central dynamic of prison life is the relationship between inmates and officers. If correctional personnel are to be more than mere custodians, they must be trained and paid in accordance with the difficulty and responsibility of their assignments. Training for correctional officers must sensitize them to understand and deal with the new breed of young inmates from the urban ghettos and to understand the racism within themselves. Above all, correctional facilities must be staffed by persons motivated to help inmates.

Forty-three people died at Attica Correctional Facility between September 9 and 13, 1971. While this riot was historical in nature, it, unfortunately, is not an isolated incident. The authors asserted in the research for this text that approximately 1,334 prison riots took place in the United States between 1900 and 1995, many of which were influenced by inmate treatment, prison conditions, managerial practices, and so forth.

After developing a proper understanding of underlying causes and trigger factors and how they manifest themselves in the prison environment, administrators will be more capable of detecting, understanding, and dealing with issues that influence institutional violence and provide practical alternatives to it. This new insight will allow the administrators of a prison the option to develop a proactive management model from which policies can be advanced when dilemmas are recognized, rather than after the damage of a riot.

Through the implementation and maintenance of enhanced security, improved communication techniques, better resource management by prison administrators, and the effective use of other riot prevention strategies as discussed in this book, such statements as those made by the Attica Commission will not become standard in the future: "Attica is every prison; and every prison is Attica" (1972, p. xii).

Bibliography

Adalist-Estrin, A. 1995. Families in Peril. *Corrections Today*. 7:116.

Adams, D., and J. Fischer. 1976. The Effects of Prison Residents' Community Contacts on Recidivism Rates. *Corrective and Social Psychiatry and Journal of Behavioral Technology Methods*. 22:21-27.

American Correctional Association. 1990a. *Causes, Preventive Measures, and Methods of Controlling Riots and Disturbances in Correctional Institutions*. Lanham, Maryland: American Correctional Association.

———. 1990b. *Standards for Adult Correctional Institutions*. Lanham, Maryland: American Correctional Association.

———. 1995. *Preventing Riots and Disturbances: A Video-based Training Course*. Lanham, Maryland: American Correctional Association.

———. 1996a. *Correctional Food Service Course*. Lanham, Maryland: American Correctional Association.

———. 1996b. *Preventing and Managing Riots and Disturbances*. Lanham, Maryland: American Correctional Association.

———. 1998. *1998 Standards Supplement*. Lanham, Maryland: American Correctional Association.

American Psychiatric Association. 1994. *Diagnostic and Statistical Manual of Mental Disorders, Fourth Edition*. Washington, D.C.: American Psychiatric Association.

Bandura, A. 1973. *Aggression: A Social Learning Analysis*. Englewood Cliffs, New Jersey: Prentice-Hall.

———. 1983. Psychological Measurement of Aggression. In R. G. Green and C. I. Donnerstein, eds. *Aggression: Theoretical and Empirical Reviews*. Volume 1. New York, New York: Academic Press.

Bandura, A., D. Ross, and S. A. Ross. 1961. Transmission of Aggression through Imitation of Aggressive Models. *Journal of Abnormal and Social Psychology*. 63:575-582.

———. 1963. Imitation of Film-mediated Aggressive Models. *Journal of Abnormal and Social Psychology*. 66:3-11.

Barak-Glantz, I. L. 1982. A Decade of Disciplinary, Administrative, and Protective Control of Prison Inmates in the Washington State Penitentiary. *Journal of Criminal Justice*. 10:481-492.

———. 1985. The Anatomy of Another Prison Riot. In M. Braswell, S. Dillingham, and R. Montgomery, Jr., eds. *Prison Violence in America*. 47-71. Cincinnati, Ohio: Anderson Publishing Company.

Baron, R. A., and D. C. Richardson. 1994. *Human Aggression, Second Edition*. New York, New York: Plenum.

Bartollas, C., and J. Conrad. 1992. *Introduction to Corrections*. New York, New York: Harper.

Berkowitz, L. 1988. Frustrations, Appraisals, and Aversively Stimulated Aggression. *Aggressive Behavior*. 14:3-11.

———. 1994a. Is Something Missing? Some Observations Prompted by the Cognitive-neoassociationist View of Anger and Emotional Aggression. In L. R. Huesmann, ed. *Aggressive Behavior: Current Perspectives*. New York: Plenum Press.

———. 1994b. Guns and Youth. In L. D. Eron, J. H. Gentry, and P. Schlegel, eds. *Reason to Hope: A Psychosocial Perspective on Violence and Youth*. Washington, D.C.: American Psychological Association.

Billy, G. D. 1996. Great Expectations of First Line Supervision. *Corrections Today*. 7:98.

Blinn, C. 1997. *Maternal Ties: A Selection of Programs for Female Offenders*. Lanham, Maryland: American Correctional Association.

Bonczar, T. 1997. *Characteristics of Adult Probation, 1995*. Washington, D.C.: Bureau of Justice Statistics.

Braswell, M., S. Dillingham, and R. Montgomery. 1985. *Prison Violence in America*. Cincinnati, Ohio: Anderson Publishing Company.

Braswell, M., R. Montgomery, and L. X. Lombardo. 1994. *Prison Violence in America*. Cincinnati, Ohio: Anderson Publishing Company.

Bright, D. E. 1951. *A Study of Institutional Impact upon Adult Male Prisoners*. Unpublished Ph.D. Dissertation, Ohio State University.

Bureau of Justice Statistics. 1997a. *Prisoners in 1996*. U.S. Department of Justice, Office of Justice Programs. June. Washington, D.C.

———. 1997b. *Lifetime Likelihood of Going to State or Federal Prison*. U.S. Department of Justice, Office of Justice Programs. Washington, D.C.

———. 1997c. *Correctional Populations in the United States, 1995: Executive Summary, 1-3*. U.S. Department of Justice, Office of Justice Programs. Washington, D.C.

Catoe, W. D. and J. L. Harvey. 1986. *A Review of the Kirkland Correctional Institution Disturbance on April 1, 1986*. Columbia, South Carolina: South Carolina Department of Corrections.

Champion, D. J. 1997. *The Roxbury Dictionary of Criminal Justice*. Los Angeles, California: Roxbury Publishing Company.

Check, J. V. P., and T. H. Guloien. 1989. Reported Proclivity for Coercive Sex Following Repeated Exposure to Sexually Violent Pornography, Nonviolent Dehumanizing Pornography, and Erotica. In D. Zillmann and J. Bryant, eds. *Pornography: Research Advances and Policy Considerations*. Hillsdale, New Jersey: Erlbaum.

Christiansen, K. and E. M. Winkler. 1992. Hormonal, Anthropometrical, and Behavioral Correlates of Physical Aggression in Kung San Men of Namibia. *Aggressive Behavior*. 18:271- 280.

Clear, T. R. and G. F. Cole. 1986. *American Corrections*. Monterey, California: Brooks/Cole Publishing Company.

Conant, R. 1968. Rioting, Instructional and Civil Disorderliness. *American Scholar*. 37:420- 433.

Corrections Compendium. 1996. Inmate Population Expected to Increase 43% by 2002. Volume XXI, April, (4). CEGA Publishing.

————. 1995. Emergency Response Teams. Volume XXI, July. 4:2-13. CEGA Publishing.

Crews, G. A., and M. R. Counts. 1997. *The Evolution of School Disturbance in America: Colonial Times to Modern Times*. Westport, Connecticut: Praeger.

Crews, G. A., R. H. Montgomery, and W. R. Garris. 1996. *Faces of Violence in America*. Needham Heights, Massachusetts: Simon & Schuster Publishing.

Czerniak, S. W. and J. R. Upchurch. 1996. Continous Improvement in Prison Security. *Corrections Today*. 4:62-64.

Dabbs, J. M., T. S. Carr, R. L. Frady, and J. K. Riad. 1995. Testosterone, Crime and Misbehavior among 692 Male Prison Inmates. *Personality and Individual Differences*. 18:627-633.

Damasio, H., T. Grabowski, R. Frank, A. M. Galaburda, and A. R. Damasio. 1994. The Return of Phineas Gage: Clues about the Brain from the Skull of a Famous Patient. *Science*. 264:1102-1105.

Davies, J. C. 1972. Toward a Theory of Revolution. In I. K. Feierabend, R. L. Feierabend, and T.R. Gurr, eds. *Prison Violence in America* (pp. 67-84). Englewood Cliffs, New Jersey: Prentice-Hall.

Desroches, F. J. 1983. Anomie, Two Theories of Prison Riots. *Canadian Journal of Criminology*. 25, 2:173-190.

Desroches, R. 1974. Patterns of Prison Riots. *Canadian Journal of Criminology and Corrections*. 16:332-351.

DiIulio, J. J. 1987. *Governing Prisons*. New York, New York: The Free Press.

Eron, L. D. 1993. Cited in T. DeAngelis. It's Back: TV Violence, Concern for Kid Viewers. *APA Monitor*. 24:16.

Eron, L., J. Gentry, and P. Schlegel. 1995. *Reason to Hope: A Psychological Perspective on Violence and Youth*. Washington, D.C.: American Psychological Association.

Farrer, B. 1995. Reducing Violence and Hostility in U.S. Corrections through the Arts. *1994 State of Corrections*. Lanham, Maryland: American Correctional Association.

Flynn, E. 1980. From Conflict Theory to Conflict Resolution: Controlling Collective Violence in Prisons. *American Behavioral Scientist*. 23:745-776.

Fox, V. 1971. Why Prisoners Riot. *Federal Probation*. 35:9-14.

———. 1972. Prison Riots in a Democratic Society. *Police*. 16:35.

Frank, L. G., S. E. Glickman, and P. Licht. 1991. Fatal Sibling Aggression, Precocial Development, and Androgens in Neonatal Spotted Hyenas. *Science*. 252:702-704.

Freeman, R. 1996. *Strategic Planning for Correctional Emergencies*. Lanham, Maryland: American Correctional Association.

Gaes, G. G. and W. J. McGuire. 1985. Prison Violence: The Contribution of Crowding Versus Other Determinants of Prison Assault Rates. *The Journal of Research in Crime and Delinquency*. 22:41-65.

Glick, B., W. Sturgeon, and C. Venator-Santiago. 1998. *No Time to Play: Youth in Adult Facilities*. Lanham, Maryland: American Correctional Association.

Gould, R. 1974. The Officer Inmate Relationship: Its Role in the Attica Rebellion. *Bulletin of the American Academy of Psychiatry and the Law*. 2, 1:34-35.

Gurr, T. R. 1972. Psychological Factors in Civil Violence. In I. K. Feierabend, R. L. Feierabend, T. R. Gurr, eds. *Collective Behavior*. 24-28. Englewood Cliffs, New Jersey: Hall.

Gutierrez-McDermid, M. Gail. 1995. Something Works: Arts in Corrections. *1994 State of Corrections*. Lanham, Maryland: American Correctional Association.

Hairston, C. F. 1988. Family Ties During Imprisonment: Do They Influence Future Criminal Activity? *Federal Probation*. 52, 1:23-29.

Henderson, J. D., W. H. Rauch, and R. L. Phillips. 1997. *Guidelines for the Development of a Security Program. Second Edition*. Lanham, Maryland: American Correctional Association.

Holt, N. and D. Miller. 1972. *Explorations in Inmates' Family Relationships*. Sacramento, California: California Department of Corrections.

Houston, J. 1995. *Correctional Management: Functions, Skills, and Systems*. Chicago, Illinois: Nelson-Hall, Inc.

Huston, A. C., E. Donnerstein, H. Fairchild, N. D. Feshbach, P. A. Katz, J. P. Murray, E. A. Rubenstein, B. L. Wilcox, and D. Zuckerman. 1992. *Big World, Small Screen: The Role of Television in American Society*. Lincoln, Nebraska: University of Nebraska Press.

Irwin, J. 1980. *Prisons in Turmoil*. Boston, Massachusetts: Little, Brown.

Jackson, G. 1970. *Soledad Brother-The Prison Letters of George Jackson*. New York, New York: Bantam Books.

Johnston, D. 1995. Care and Placement of Prisoners' Children. In K. Gabel and D. Johnston, eds. *Children of Incarcerated Parents*. Boston, Massachusetts: Lexington Books.

Knox, G. W. and E. D. Tromhanauser. 1991. Gangs and Their Control in Adult Correctional Institutions. *The Prison Journal*. 71(2)15-22.

Lauen, R. J. 1997. *Positive Approaches to Corrections: Research, Policy, and Practice*. Lanham, Maryland: American Correctional Association.

Lefkowitz, M. M., L. D. Eron, L. O. Walder, and L. R. Huesmann. 1977. *Growing Up to Be Violent: A Longitudinal Study of the Development of Aggression*. New York, New York: Pergamon Press.

Leopold, N. F. 1958. *Life Plus 99 Years*. New York, New York: Doubleday Publishing.

Levinson, Robert B. 1994. Prison Gangs: A National Assessment. *1994 State of Corrections*. Lanham, Maryland: American Correctional Association.

Loeber, R. and D. Hay. 1997. Key Issues in the Development of Aggression and Violence from Childhood to Early Adulthood. *Annual Review of Psychology*. 48:371-410.

MacDougall, E. and R. Montgomery. 1986. Curing Criminals. *The Futurist*. 36-37.

Mahan, S. 1985. An 'Orgy of Brutality' at Attica and the 'Killing Ground' at Santa Fe. In M. Braswell, S. Dillingham, and R. Montgomery, Jr., eds. *Prison Violence in America*. 73-78. Cincinnati, Ohio: Anderson Publishing Company.

Martin, R. and S. Zimmerman. 1990. A Typology of the Causes of Prison Riots and an Analytical Extension to the 1986 West Virginia Riot. *Justice Quarterly*. 7, 4:711-737.

McConville, S. 1985. *Prison Gangs*. Symposium conducted at the annual meeting of the Mid-Western Criminal Justice Association.

McCuen, S. E. 1968. Guards Quickly Put Down Prison Inmate Disturbance. *The State*. Columbia, South Carolina. April 2.

McMains, M. J., and W. C. Mullens. 1996. *Crisis Negotiations: Managing Critical Incidents and Hostage Situations in Law Enforcement and Corrections*. Cincinnati, Ohio: Anderson Publishing Company.

Miller, J. M. and J. P. Rush. 1996. *Gangs: A Criminal Justice Approach*. Anderson Publishing Company.

Morris, R. 1983. *The Devil's Butcher Shop*. Albuquerque, New Mexico: University of New Mexico Press.

National Institute of Corrections. 1982. *Containment of Prison Violence*. Washington, D.C.: National Institute of Corrections.

New York State Special Commission on Attica. 1972. *The Official Report of the New York State Special Commission on Attica*. New York, New York: Bantam Books, Inc.

Nordstrom, P. and M. Asberg. 1992. Suicide Risk and Serotonin. *International Clinical Psychopharmacology*. 6:2-21.

Ohlin, L. E. 1951. *Selection for Parole*. New York, New York: Russell Sage Foundation.

Polusny, M. A. and V. M. Folletee. 1995. Long-term Correlates of Child Abuse: Theory and Review of the Empirical Literature. *Applied and Preventive Psychology*. 4:143-166.

Porporino, F. J. 1986. Managing Violent Individuals in Correctional Settings. *Journal of Interpersonal Violence*. 1:213-237.

Powell, D. A., S. L. Buchanan, and C. M. Gibbs. 1990. Role of the Prefrontal-thalamic Axis in Classical Conditioning. In H. B. M. Uylings, C. G. Van Eden, J. P. C. De Bruin, M. A. Corner, and M. G. P. Feenstra, eds. *Progress in Brain Research*. Volume 85. The Prefrontal Cortex: Its Structure, Function and Pathology. Amsterdam: Elsevier.

Roberts, J. W. 1997. *Reform and Retribution: An Illustrated History of American Prisons*. Lanham, Maryland: American Correctional Association.

Rose, R. J. 1995. Genes and Human Behavior. *Annual Review of Psychology*. 46:625-664.

Rostad, Knut A. and L. R. Witke. 1997. Silence is Golden. *Corrections Today*. 2:91-92.

Saudou, F., D. A. Amara, M. C. Buhot, A. Dierich, R. Hen, M. Lemeur, S. Ramboz, and L. Segu. 1994. Enhanced Aggressive Behavior in Mice Lacking 5-HT1B Receptor. *Science*. 265:1875-1878.

Schwartz, M. C., and J. F. Weintraub. 1974. The Prisoner's Wife: A Study in Crisis. *Federal Probation*. 26:20-26.

Senese, J. D. 1994. Use of Force in America's Prisons: An Overview of Current Research. *Corrections Today*. 4:112.

Siever, L., and R. L. Trestman. 1993. The Serotonin System and Aggressive Personality Disorder. *International Clinical Psychopharmacology*. 8, 2:33-39.

Silberman, M. 1995. *A World of Violence*. Belmont, California: Wadsworth Publishing Company.

Skovron, S. E. 1988. Prison Crowding: The Dimensions of the Problem and Strategies of Population Control. *Controversial Issues in Crime and Justice*. 183-198.

Smelser, N. J. 1963. *Theory of Collective Behavior*. New York, New York: The Free Press.

Smith, A. E. 1973. The Conflict Theory of Riots. In South Carolina Department of Corrections. *Collective Violence in Correctional Institutions; A Search for Causes*. 34-36. Columbia, South Carolina: State Printing Company.

South Carolina. 1923. *Report of the Special Joint Legislative Committee to Investigate Conditions at the State Penitentiary*. Volume II.

South Carolina Department of Corrections. 1973. *Collective Violence in Correctional Institutions: A Search for Causes*. Columbia, South Carolina: State Printing Company.

Stojkivic, S. and R. Lovell. 1992. *Corrections: An Introduction*. Cincinnati, Ohio: Anderson Publishing Company.

Sykes, G. 1958. *The Society of Captives: A Study of a Maximum Security Prison*. Princeton, New Jersey: Princeton University Press.

Tellegen, A., D. T. Lykken, T. J. Bouchard, K. J. Wilcox, N. L. Segal, and S. Rich. 1988. Personality Similarity in Twins Reared Apart and Together. *Journal of Personality and Social Psychology*. 54:1031-1039.

Toch, H. 1977. *Living in Prison: The Ecology of Survival*. New York, New York: The Free Press.

Triandis, H. C. 1994. Culture and Social Behavior. New York, New York: McGraw Hill.

U.S. House of Representatives. 1973. *Report by the Select Committee on Crime*. House Report No. 93-329. 93rd Congress. Washington, D.C.: U.S. Government Printing Office.

Useem, B. and P. Kimball. 1991. *States of Siege: U.S. Prison Riots 1971-1986*. New York, New York: Oxford University Press.

Uylings, H. B. M., C. G. Van Eden, J. P. C. De Bruin, and M. P. G. Feenstra, eds. 1990. *Progress in Brain Research*. Volume 85. The Prefrontal Cortex: Its Structure, Function and Pathology. Amsterdam: Elsevier.

Virkkunen, M. and M. Linnoila. 1993. Brain Serotonin, Type II Alcoholism and Impulsive Violence. *Journal of Studies on Alcohol*. 11:163-169.

Warthen, B. 1997. School Discipline Takes More than Deputies. *The State*. Columbia, South Carolina. October 27.

Widom, C. S. 1989. Does Violence Beget Violence? A Critical Examination of the Literature. *Psychological Bulletin*. 106:3-28.

Witke, L. 1998. How to Identify and Evaluate Technology in Corrections. *1997 State of Corrections*. Lanham, Maryland: American Correctional Association.

Young, W. and M. Brown. 1993. Cross-national Comparisons of Imprisonment. *Crime and Justice: A Review of Research*. 17:1-49.

Index

Municipal police department, notification
of, 125

N

National Guard, notification of, 125
National Survey of Prison Riots   (1984) 3, 9,
(1996) 4, 9
Nebraska
Nebraska Center for Women, 40
Nebraska State Penitentiary, 23
riots in state, 76
Negotiation, as end to riot, 78-79
Neurotransmitters, xiv
Nevada
riots in state, 76
State Prison, 25
New Hampshire
riots in state, 76
Stafford County Jail, 30
New Jersey
Bayside State Prison, 35
Essex County Jail, 59
Rahway State Prison, 60
riots in state, 76
New Mexico
New Mexico State Penitentiary, 19, 23,
133-34
Penitentiary of New Mexico in Santa
Fe, 61
riots in state, 76
New York
Altona, 19
Attica. *See* Attica
Auburn Prison, 48, 58
Bedford Reformatory for Women, 12-13
Bronx County Jail, 16
Elmira Correctional Facility, 117
Metropolitan Correctional Center, 56
riots in state, 76, 77, 83
Sing Sing Prison, 57-58
Tombs, 48
Noise levels, 42, 106, 100, 111

North Carolina
Cameron-Morrison Youth
Institution, 38, 65
Central Prison, 11, 58-59
Correctional Center for Women, 18
McDowell County Unit, 22
North Carolina Women's Prison, 30
riots in state, 76
North Dakota, 76

O

Ohio
Chillicothe Reformatory, 11
Lucasville, 65
Ohio Penitentiary, 11
riots in state, 76
Oklahoma
Joe Harp Correctional Center, 62
Mack Alford Correctional Center, 14
riots in state, 76
Ombudsperson, 114
Operational capacity
defined, 100
Oregon State Penitentiary in Salem, 44, 58
inmate population increase in, 105
riots in state, 76
Oswald, R., 59
Overcrowding, 42, 66, 103, 106
and riots, 82
at Attica, 55
Bell v. Wolfish. See Bell v. Wolfish
capacity measures, 100
factor of tension and stress, 110
in state prisons, 99-100

P

Patrols, 36
Pennsylvania
Allegheny County Prison, 29
Camp Hill Correctional Institution, 64
Holmesburg State Prison, 39
Huntingdon, 19

About the Authors

Dr. Reid H. Montgomery, Jr. is an associate professor in the College of Criminal Justice at the University of South Carolina and coauthor of six books. He joined the University of South Carolina faculty after service as a federal probation officer with the U.S. District Court in Washington, D.C., under Chief Judge John J. Sirica. Prior to graduate study, he served on active duty with the Third Infantry (Old Guard) at Ft. Myer, Virginia. He has a B.S., M.Ed., and Ph.D. from the University of South Carolina, where his dissertation analyzed attitudes leading to prison riots. Named in 1984 as Educator of the Year by the Southern Association of Criminal Justice Educators, Dr. Montgomery has pursued postdoctoral study at George Washington University in Washington, D.C.

Dr. Gordon A. Crews is presently the Director of Criminal Justice and Military Programs at the University of South Carolina Beaufort. He was formerly a faculty member in the Social and Behavioral Sciences Department of Midlands Technical College in Columbia, South Carolina, where he taught courses in police administration, corrections, criminology, and ethics. He earned a Ph.D. in Elementary Education, a Graduate Certificate in Alcohol and Drug studies, and a Bachelor of Science and Masters degrees in Criminal Justice from the University of South Carolina. Prior to teaching, Dr. Crews worked in law enforcement as a bloodhound officer and trainer, field training officer, and criminal investigator; in corrections as a training and accreditation manager; and in insurance fraud as an investigator. His publications include journal articles dealing with school violence, satanic involvement and youth, and law enforcement issues. His most recent books are *Faces of Violence in America* (1996), published by Simon & Schuster and *The Evolution of School Disturbance in America: Colonial Times to Modern Day* (1997), published by Praeger Publishing.

Contributing Writers

William R. Crawley assisted in the research and writing of this text. He is currently a graduate student at the University of South Carolina, Columbia. He is completing a Masters of Criminal Justice, as well as a Graduate Certificate in Drug and Alcohol studies. His current academic specialization includes criminological theory, international crime, and forensic psychology. He also holds a Bachelor of Science in

Resource Management/Consumer Science (Iowa State University) and a Bachelor of Arts in Asian Studies: Japanese (University of Iowa). In addition, he studied in Yamato-shi, Japan during the summer of 1996 and has written extensively on Asian organized crime and law enforcement.

Dr. Charles M. Gibbs was awarded a Bachelor of Science in Psychology at the University of Illinois in 1971. He earned both an M. A. (1976) and his Ph.D. (1979) in biopsychology at the University of Iowa. Dr. Gibbs served as a postdoctoral fellow/associate in the field of neurobiology and behavior at the University of Virginia (1979) and the State University of New York, Stony Brook (1979-1984), where he conducted research pertaining to the biological bases of learning and memory. Beginning in 1985, Dr. Gibbs established an electrophysiology laboratory at the W. J. B. Dorn Veterans' Hospital in Columbia, South Carolina, where he continued his research on the basic brain mechanisms involved in associative learning and memory. His research efforts have led to the publication of many articles, which have provided fruitful insights into the respective roles of the prefrontal cortex, cerebellum, and related brain structures in Pavlovian conditioning processes. Until his retirement from science in 1995, Dr. Gibbs was heavily involved with the local neuroscience community in Columbia, and he is a past-president of the South Carolina Chapter of the Society for Neuroscience. Dr. Gibbs currently is fulfilling a long-standing dream of educating young minds through his academic role at Midlands Technical College in Columbia, South Carolina, where he teaches courses in the areas of the science of psychology, abnormal psychology, and behavior modification.